Down the River

DOWN the RIVER

— BY —

H·E·BATES

illustrated by
PETER PARTINGTON

LONDON
VICTOR GOLLANCZ LTD
1987

First published in Great Britain 1937
by Victor Gollancz Ltd,
14 Henrietta Street, London WC2E 8QJ,
with illustrations by Agnes Miller Parker

This newly illustrated edition first published 1987

British Library Cataloguing in Publication Data
Bates, H. E.
    Down the river.
    1. Great Ouse, River, Region (England)—
    Description and travel 2. Nene, River,
    Region (England)—Description and travel
    I. Title
    942.5   DA670.G7/

ISBN 0-575-03885-2

Printed in Spain

Contents

The Twin Rivers

I count it one of the luckiest things in life to have been born within reach of a river valley: not in it, nor above it, but just so far removed from it that it never became a too familiar sight and never quite ceased to be a wonder. A man born on a hill must look down on the world; a man born in a valley must look up to it. We, on the other hand, had neither to look up nor down. Standing on flat but raised ground, we looked across and about us; we saw things squarely, at a proper distance, on a proper plane, in a proper perspective. And that gave us perhaps, in that district, the sturdy independence for which we were noted.

But I had more luck. I was born not only within reach of one river valley, but two. I could almost reach out, with my two hands, and touch those twin but quite dissimilar streams flowing on almost parallel courses to the North Sea. Tired of one, I could go to the other. On the Nene I could watch the traffic of barges I could never see on the Ouse; on the Ouse I could see a richness of flower life that the Nene, being navigated, could not offer. On both and by both I could watch birds: herons flapping up with a kind of gaunt grandeur from the more solitary bits of marsh, many swans and many thousands of seagulls in the winter acres of floods, kingfishers and coot and moorhens and wild duck and snipe and, most rarely, wild geese creaking and honking over in snow-grey skeins or pairs against a snow-grey sky. In both I tried, and failed, to catch fish: thus disgracing the traditions of a family whose more notorious members were, so to speak, born with rods in their hands. On both I watched butterflies, saw dragonflies perform that miracle of emergence on still water surfaces among water-lilies at high summer: thus preserving, in a small way, the traditions of a family whose less notorious members knew more about the world of butterflies than the average man knows about the world of race-horses. On and by these rivers, also, I boated and bathed and skated and nested and, not least, did much dreaming and some courting. To one, the Ouse, I had nothing and needed nothing to attract me except its own placid but rich life; it was an idyllic and generous stream, flowery, unnavigated, watering a lovely valley. The other, the Nene, could offer me not merely an exciting life, but a life that had been and gone; it was a prosaic stream, flowerless, navigated, watering what was very often an ugly valley, but it had carried a rich traffic of life, during the late nineteenth century, that it no longer knew—the wild traffic of barges and bargees, the swaggering rough stuff of boozers and fancy but not too fancy ladies in the river-side pubs, the betting and boasting and comedy and often tragedy of hot summer evenings when the beer was served outside, under the chestnut trees, the sly slippery stuff of river-poachers, of eel-trappers, of night work. It was not merely a river; it was a history. I listened to its stories. They re-created for me not only a life

I had not known but a life, as I knew later, that would not return.

These two rivers were, therefore, like breasts which suckled me. I drew from them a lot that was best in boyhood; and in memory they still nourish me. For the best thing about a river is its permanence. You may grow up to cherish a memory of the house in which you were born, only to find, in ten, twenty or thirty years, that circumstances have knocked it down; you may cling to the remembrance of a wood or a field or a garden or a single tree or even a road, only to find that time or circumstance or the local authority had changed it or effaced it altogether. But rivers, like hills and the sea, defy the most catastrophic changes. They are indestructible. They have something immutable and eternal about them. If a tree or a wood or a house stand in the way of man, he can, for very little expense, remove them. But if a river stands in the way there is nothing for it but to build, at very great expense, a bridge. The river triumphs. And, since it is not only indestructible but a thing of destruction itself, it also terrifies. Then again, since it not only destroys but is a means to the creation of life and beauty, it also soothes and stimulates. It is at once a thing of wildness and tranquillity, of motion and stillness, of music and silence, of life and solitude, of simplicity and secrecy, of idyllicism and tragedy. It is a complete world. It has not only its own special life but it attracts an astonishingly diverse life from other things and places: from the sea and towns, from the roads and sky, from woods and fields. A river has all the advantages of a road except that it will not carry motor-cars; it shares the best of the sea's life without the worst of its terrors; it has much in common with woods; and since meadows and towns come down to its banks it gives and borrows life from them too. The river, in fact, having a highly individual and unique life of its own into the bargain, scores every time. The best of a country's history is written on its rivers.

For me, water attracts like a magnet. I not only boated and fished and dreamed and courted in and on two rivers, but I fell in them. I not only fell in them but in their tributaries, even in the springs which fed them. I could not reach for a branch of crab-blossom without overbalancing and sitting in a trout pool, trousers having subsequently to be dried on the twigs of a hawthorn. I could not

fish for stickleback without the bank subsiding and letting me in, trousers having to be dried again. I could not jump a brook, though I was a good jumper, without some mysterious magnetism pulling me down when I was half way over. I could not even gather water-cress or wild iris or search for eggs in marshy places without stepping on what looked like dry land but which was, in reality, a pool that came over my knees. Water attracts me as women attract men, as cherries attract blackbirds. I fall for it every time.

And, as I hope these pages will show, I fall for it still. Water has some kind of powerful mystery about it. Still waters, moving waters, dark waters: the words themselves have a mysterious, almost a dying fall. Roads, meadows, towns, gardens, woods are man-made; a river is a primeval piece of work. It is ageless but, at the same time, perpetually young. It travels, but remains. It is a paradox of eternal age and eternal youth, of change and changelessness, of permanence and transience. And if there is, perhaps, a dogmatic flavour about these remarks it is comforting to reflect that they will be true, roughly, barring astronomical accidents, in ten thousand years.

A Boy's Brook

As a boy I used to spend half my days on a high piece of farmland, arable mostly, with stiff hawthorn hedges and iron-grey ash trees criss-crossing and dotting the same sort of land for miles about. From that point, on fine days, if we were lucky, we could count the spires of nine churches. We saw, on days of extra good visibility, the light on distant water towers and the drift of smoke from brick-yard chimneys. At night, if it were clear, we saw the crimson, almost ferocious glow of distant furnaces. But all day and every day, winter and summer, rain or fine, we could see something else. We could not miss it. It lay just below us, a dozen fields away, a mythical stone's throw, running like a steel snake through illimitable green acres of meadowland. It was the Nene, flowing down to the Wash.

It is, as its name says, a river of nine sources. I did not know one of them but I knew a tenth. And that small spring, gushing out from under the raw elbow roots of a clump of cow-smoothed hawthorns, still remains for me not only the source of the Nene, though it never was, but the source of all rivers at all. It was a beautiful spring, coming up suddenly in a shadowy place, on a slope, and it was an extraordinary colour. It ran like blood. More truly, it ran out like the long flow of a girl's red hair: a savage auburn red, a kind of bloody rust that stained the bank and spread and oozed and silted all over the marsh at the foot of the slope, crimsoning the water-cresses, bloodying the iris-roots and grass and sedge, scumming in small pools, running occasionally as clear as wine, spreading like a fine red varnish down the steep bank of the brook, to be diluted and lost at last. Yet, when you cupped the water itself, it lay in the hand as clear as glass, only infinitesimally specked with motes of iron-stone.

"And by gummy, I bet that's good for folks, ain't it?" my grandfather would say. "Iron? I bet that water'd cure any mortal thing, wouldn't it? Dall it, if we could git anew bottles and bottle it and sell it we could make money."

"That's what we ought to do."

"You ever heard talk o' those places where old gals sit and drink water for rheumatics? Well, I bet this is one o' them springs, ain't it? If we could git anew bottles we could make thousands."

"Well, why don't we?" I'd say. "If we could get the bottles I could sit here all day and fill 'em and you could bring the old pony down every night when it got dark and we could take 'em away."

Yes, that was all we ever had to do: bottle that water and fetch it away with the old pony and trap and sell it and make money. But somehow we never did. Something else always cropped up: the sow was in pig, or it was harvest or haymaking or seed-time, or the nag needed shoeing. Somehow we never bottled that life-giving water. But that, my grandfather would point out, was the way of life. Here was Nature providing all that was ever wanted to cure every kind of ill that flesh was heir to, and man took no notice.

Take a thing like herbs. "Boy," he'd say to me as we prowled along that brook, "boykin, I'd don't care what it is—coughs, colds, bellyache, rheumatics, wind—I don't care what it is, there's a herb to cure it. You think these things was put here for nothing? These herbs? Look at hound's-tongue. Look at the ointment that makes. I bet there ain't nothing in the nation world hound's-tongue won't cure."

Yes, look at hound's-tongue. That was another thing we were going to make fortunes from but never did. All we had to do was to boil enough hound's-tongue and enough lard in order to make enough ointment, and finally enough money. Ointment that would cure anything. Boils. Tumours. Cancers. Sores. Bad legs. Chilblains. Black eyes. Festers. Everything. It was, it ought to have been, the wonder of the world. I saw it marketed, advertised. "Lucas and Bates Sovereign Cure-All for all Cases." And once: "Prof. Bates's Miracle Ointment—Soothes all Sores—Pulverises all Pains." Ointment and alliteration were going to conquer the world and make my fortune. And why not? Fortunes have been made on alliteration alone.

But I was serious. By day I mooched along that brook-side and searched for herbs. By night I read Culpeper. A strange book. There was much in it I did not understand. Take lettuce. "Being eaten boiled it opens the bowels; promotes digestion, quenches thirst, increaseth milk in nurses, easeth griping pains in the stomach and bowels that come of choler, abateth bodily lust." Take dog's mercury. "The decoction, made with water and a cock chicken, is a most safe medicine for hot fits of agues." Take thoroughwax. "It being applied with a little flour and wax to children's navels that stick out, it reduces them." There was much in it about spleen and travail, phrenzy and lethargy, the veins and the courses, the stone and the choler. For myself I went for things I understood. I gathered yarrow. It was good for toothache. I boiled the roots of elm. The juice was a hair-restorer. I stewed the roots of mallow. They banished coughs, hoarseness, shortness of breath and wheezings. I spent hours with that book. I studied venery, vertigo, vomiting, worms, windiness, wombs, melancholy, the mother, jaundice, leprosy, loss of voice, palsy, pin and web, St. Anthony's fire, surfeits, swellings, swoonings, in short, everything. I could have passed examinations in it. But the trouble was not to pass examinations, but to find people who had venery, vertigo, vomiting and the rest. I had the cures. What I lacked was the patients.

And that, combined with something else, finally drove me out of business. The something else was the economics of the thing. It was all very well to talk of the free bounty of nature, but it took six hours hard gas-cooking to stew enough hair-oil to cure one bald patch, even supposing it cured at all. Again, I got no support. None of my family were bald and I never got a chance. For a long time I kept the bottles of hair-oil in the washstand drawer, looked at them every night and hoped and wondered. "Bates's Brilliantine," I was going to call it. Suddenly it began to give off a strange odour. Then it fermented. It worked up like pink beer. Even then I still believed in it. Then it stank. That was the end.

Or rather it was the end of the herbs, but not the brook. As so often happens, I went out to find one thing, missed it and found another. I cannot remember now what cures the palsy or what eases the choleric belchings, but I do not need even to shut my eyes in order to remember every detail of the reaches of that small stream. I wandered up and down it in all weathers, at all seasons. It came down fairly fast, winding, always narrow, with occasional black pools and occasional shallows of white stone and sand. It was overhung, almost everywhere, with haw and hazel and ash and wild-rose and willow, so that it was always shadowy. Winding, cut off into sections by the tall hedges of the fields running at right-angles to it, it had some quality of unexpected and mysterious attraction. Beyond each bend was another. Beyond each field was another. They were all different. And the stream was like some long flowing magnet that drew you farther and farther up the reaches, beyond the known places. It had a great harvest of flower life, some fish, many birds. In places the small meadows had been turned by neglect into small marshes. They bristled with sedge and rush and, in rare places, giant reeds that stood all winter long like great fawn ostrich feathers which the wind shivered and flapped and rattled with harsh noises. Those reeds, in winter, gave the place a forlorn air, a feeling of almost wild solitude. In summer nothing could have been more tranquil. The reeds stood like giant corn; the great hawthorn hedges, never cut for years, shut out the world; the sedge and the brook-sides were starred and pricked with small forests of water forget-me-not and willow herb. It was all quiet, idyllic, lost, marvellously tranquil, incomparable. Nobody ever went there. The fishing was gone; there was no shooting; it was bad country for horses. A cowman would come down, perhaps, in the early afternoon, holloping and hawking for the herd, and the cows would squelch up and a dog would bark, but they were, generally, all the sounds of the outside world we ever

heard there. The stream itself made scarcely any sound at all: only that tinkling-linkling, almost gently metallic, almost singing sound as it curdled on stones in shallow places. It had no waterfalls, no bits of foaming and crashing chorus. All the best of its beauty lay in its quietness, in its absolute tranquillity of sound and colouring and movement and scene. It was best in summer, when quietness and sound and sun and colours fused about it like a breath: lying in the shade of its big hawthorns I would watch, then, the last of its fish-life, the pike gone and the roach and gudgeon with them, and now only the small schools of small trout remaining. They lay, generally, in sunlight, above stones, in the clear reaches that were no deeper than a child's ankle. They were like fish-ghosts, platooned, shadowy, still as death, no more than the shadows of willow-leaves until some muscle of the current moved and turned them gently over and flicked them back again, in a flash of silver. There had, once, been considerable pike, in deep reaches and currentless backwaters, but though they grew in size, as fish will, long after they were dead, I think they were mostly jack. I watched, but never saw them. My grandfather had in the past often snared them, and he liked to persuade me, as fishermen do, that he was an expert. He would lie on his belly in some quiet place and let down the snare an inch or two in front of the jack's nose and wait until he struck and then strike too. Now I think of it, the stream had eels also, and he would take them with night-lines. But somewhere between those days and mine something had happened: the stream had changed its course. The backwaters had dried up, the pike reaches had gone. And though I would not have changed for anything the stream as I knew it I would like to have seen it as it once was, a sort of double stream, with long islands of grass made by the tree-hung backwaters, with much fish and a wealth of snipe and kingfisher and even, perhaps, otter. It would have been a wilder stream, in keeping with a wilder century.

As I knew it, its life was unspectacular: no otters, no pike, kingfishers rarely, snipe more rarely still. Voles would plop down and vanish and rise again and then disappear at all times of the year, that sudden plop in the water a startling sound in the stillness. Wild duck would scare up, always distant, from the forests of reed feathers. Herons patrolled up and down, looking vast and sombre, and always, almost every day, we saw that intense miracle of hovering by some solitary sparrow-hawk, far up, fixed against the sky with a kind of savage immobility, performing that miraculous trick of hunting by hypnotism, of killing by that merciless stillness that is not stillness at all. And once, without warning, I was startled by the uprising from the reed-feathers of some giant bird, a goose most likely, a gigantic ghost that struggled up with powerful clumsiness, its wings rowing like great oars, its slow-motion flight up the valley gloomy and fascinating and impressive. And once, too, and thank heaven, only once, I came upon the nicest bevy of duck feeding among the sedge and water-cress of a strip of marsh. Now I had never seen wild duck before, and this was the handsomest, fattest brood I could ever hope to see. I knew, roughly, what wild duck should look like, and the only thing that really troubled me about these duck was that they were all a delicate fawn in colour. But then, no doubt, the species varied, and what were they doing here, anyway, in this lonely marsh, more than a mile from the nearest house, if they were not wild? So I stalked them, squelching and slithering and sinking in that oily marsh until, as I thought, I had them set. And then suddenly I tore forth in desperate chase. Every duck squawked and quacked and flapped about in mad terror. I chased them for half an hour. The thing that I couldn't then fathom, but which I have fathomed very often since, was that not a solitary duck troubled to fly. They simply quacked and flopped. And somehow that quacking and flopping wasn't quite wild enough for me. It seemed domestic. And suddenly I realised it was domestic. In that instant I turned to set up what were, for me, new cross-country records.

Farther up the stream there were ducks about which I had no doubts: ducks of decent domestic whiteness. At that village, sprinkled all along the stream-side, half the population, I think, kept ducks. So I could see there two of the things which delight me most in village life: a stream crossing the village street and on it an endless patrolling and procession of ducks. There, at that point, stone walls and houses and grass and duck and water and wood-land fused to make a scene that was almost too idyllic. It was that scene with which, in the eighteenth century, and still more in the nineteenth, third-rate engravers embellished the title pages of third-rate poets. It was pastoral, lyrical, a scene observed and

drawn with half-closed eyes. I see it still, but not quite like that. I see the stream coming from under the dark kingfisher-reaches out into the light, spreading and tippling over the road, turning under the bridges, washing the white flat stepping-stones, catching the ducks in sudden currents and, at flood-time, sudden whirlpools that sent them spinning downstream like bits of comic clockwork. I see all that, but I see also the greenish duck-turds on the water's edge, the curled floating duck feathers, the print of ducks' feet in the washed-up mud, and it is the ducks and the memory also of snake-lines of golden ducklings fluffed by spring winds that give the scene its life. Water will change the whole aspect of a landscape, but ducks in turn will change the whole aspect of water. Any photographer would give his head for a line of ducks at the right place in the right light at the right time. Ducks give to a scene something not quite idyllic, not quite comic. They are the absurdest, oddest, most lovable of birds. They are symbols of comedy everywhere. No bird with a voice so cracked and fatuous could hope to be taken seriously. Yet those ducks, on that small stream, at the point where it washed over the road and vanished fieldwards again among summer forests of brook-lime and willow herb, have for me a charm and regality not surpassed, even by swans, by any other bird anywhere.

Just beyond the province of these ducks the stream, for me, went no further. I never even hankered to know it beyond that point, where, at the foot of a hill, it went across the road again. Time had put up there a thick barricade of haw and rose and willow herb that cut me off from its upper reaches. Man had put up a small white bridge. It was a rounding off, a completion, a fulfilment. The stream ended.

But if it ended it also began. From that bridge I did all that was worth while to a child: fished and paddled, gathered cresses and flowers, ran for dragonflies, cupped my hands and drank. In winter, at threshing-time, and in summer, in times of drought, I took a cart there for water. Winter and summer I let the horse stand up to his hocks and drink, myself sitting on the cart in midstream, with the odd feeling of being in some high strange-fangled ship. And there also, winter and summer, but in summer most, I lay or sat or stood and did what is the best of all things to do by the side of water—nothing at all. I would lie and absorb, unconsciously, the heart of summer: the great depth of July heat, the small sounds of water, the click of insects, the monotonous phrases of yellow-hammers uttered as though in a dream, the chimes from the church on the little hill above, the drowsy scent of water-mint and water and earth and sun that was like an anæsthetic.

It was the best of all possible occupations in the best of all possible worlds. I varied it, sometimes, by that other universal pursuit. I threw into the water boats of straw and paper, of wood and leaves, even of wool and flowers. I dropped them in and watched and wondered if they would ever get to the sea.

The First River

We went to the brook on all days of the week; we kept the river for Sundays. Only on that day, it seemed, could we pay it the proper leisurely homage it deserved. The brook we could scramble along, adventurously, carelessly, alone in its solitary reaches. We thought of it, though it did not belong to us, as exclusive to ourselves. We gathered its cresses by the sackful, we talked of bottling its waters, we resented intruders. It had nothing social about it. It was a small wild world, secret and separate.

Whereas the river was communal. We could not think, and never dreamed, of claiming it as our own. It was something public and important. It was maintained by a navigation company. It had traffic, mills, locks, towpaths, fine stone bridges, landing wharves. There was no chance, except at dead of night, of being alone on it. It was not merely a piece of water. It was a highway, a meeting-place, a unit of power. People had rights in it: fishing rights, traffic rights and so on. Lovers and fishermen were jealous of it; men who had lived all their lives within call of its banks drowned themselves in it. It was a place in which there was not only the play of wild life, but the play of human life. The brook was secret, merry, jingling, unspectacular, a mere lyric of a stream. The river had some quality of benign universality, of immense and almost magnetic mystery. If we had lacked a god, it would have been no bad thing to worship.

For myself, there was no doubt at all that I did worship it. That Sunday excursion, made invariably in the evenings, in summer, was a piece of ritual; we walked at a solemn pace, easily, reverently, shoes squeaking, collars circumspect. No running about, no jumping of dykes, no hedge-clambering for nests or blossoms, only an easy pilgrimage to one end and one god, the river.

We began, usually, after tea, about five o'clock. Always there was that curious Sunday hush over everything, a kind of woollen pall, almost uncanny, an expansive and benign silence broken only, perhaps, by the sound of pianos trying over hymns in the parlours of the devout or ragtimes in the front rooms of the irreverent. At that hour people were not stirring. We walked through the single empty street that led us to the river lane with a feeling that, somehow, we were too early, that the performance was not yet due to begin. There was something suspended and uplifted and almost unnatural about that strange Sunday silence. We tuned our pace to it. My grandfather looked at his watch, as though in a fear that we might exceed some spiritual speed limit; he looked at the sky, with some remark that it was, in his opinion, all over alike in patches, or that not a leaf moved or that it was, generally, a bit thick in the clear; we passed under the shade of the vast walnut tree that was like a gateway between town and country, and a moment later by the small stone house where he, and fifty years afterwards my wife, was born; and the pilgrimage had begun.

It was a crazy lane, nothing but a track in summer, dried mud worn and scarred and ridged by the passage of thousands of cows and men going up and down there from town to river, through countless generations. "Walk straight, walk properly!" How the devil, indeed, could I walk straight? That track had one thing in common with death: it levelled all men. It made them all drunk. For me, a boy, the ridge steps made and used by ages of cows were just too short to take in one stride and, damnably, just too wide to take in two. Even a long-legged man got tangled. And where there were no ridges and the passage of cows had gone into disorder, the great cow-prints, sunk down and baked like iron, were a torture. So we were forced on to the narrow path of men, to walk as decently, often in Indian file, as the day demanded.

I say walked. I should say progressed; I should say, perhaps, that we advanced in a series of progressions. If it is better to travel than to arrive, it was evidently, in the opinion of my grandfather, better to stand still than to travel at all. We were the perfect exponents of Davies' poem. For every five minutes of progression, we had, I think, ten of standing and staring. We stopped for anything, a crop of wheat rising to ear, a kingfisher, a magpie, a host of butterflies, a sound, a change of light. "Stop a minute. Ye hear that? Hold hard. Ye see that? What is it? What was it?" We paused to observe the sky, the shape of a cloud, the promise of distances. Would it rain? Did it thunder? We stopped to catch the scent of things, of mown wheat, of honeysuckle, of invisible fields of flowering beans. We were arrested by the sudden sight of herons, of wind waving the grass. We stopped to turn a stone of queer shape, to pick it up and feel it and wonder. We lingered to praise and criticise. We paused for blackberries, to wonder when the sloe-crop would be ripe, to give an opinion on oats and hay. We stopped—as though it were ever necessary—to rest, to look about us, to take stock, to spit, to make water. We stopped for the sheer simple luxurious pleasure of stopping. But most of all, and most often of all, we stopped to talk with other men.

"Evenin', George. By God, ain't it nation hot?"

"Rare weather."

Then, after such introductory exchanges, there would be a kind of settling down, an easing of breeches, a gradual tuning of thought. The conversation would touch on trivialities, or deepen or perish. It might be secret. "Well, I ain't sayin' it will and I ain't sayin' it won't, but if you're outside the Dragon at seven tomorrow night, well——" It might become political, earnest. We lived in a rum world, a world of jiggery-pokery governed by a bunch of humbugs in Parliament. Did you ever hear of anything in all your born days like the bastards were doing now? It became domestic, horticultural. It was the age of buttonholes, when men were not ashamed to wear in their lapels cabbage roses and bouquets of sweet peas and, about harvest time, in their caps, those straw loveknots, delicately twisted, that have long since gone out of fashion. We admired a man's buttonhole; my grandfather asked for the name of a rose. We were given its history, promised cuttings. Hours passed. It was all leisurely, pleasant, timeless: a drowsily tranquil world hedged in by great hedges of elder and haw, a world drenched by the scent of hay and honeysuckle, of wheat and sun, of cows and rain. And how's wheat going to pan out? And how's Albert? And who's this?

"Who's this? Wur, this is Lizzie's boy."

"By God, it ain't, is it? I never knowed him. Shoots up, don't he?"

"Bless y' heart an' life, shoots up, he's just won a scholarship."

"Scholarship? Never such a thing in me life. Scholarship. Things are different, now, ain't they? We never had scholarships."

"Learns French."

"Learns French? Wonder what the hell they'll learn 'em next?"

And all the time I, listening and pretending often not to listen, was learning something which all the teachers of French in the world could not have taught me. The accent and look and feeling and colour of country people and things were being pressed on my mind, though I did not know it, with imperishable indelibility. My ears were cocked. And in that lane, on those Sunday evenings, I absorbed things which cannot be reckoned at all by material values. I absorbed whole worlds and histories.

There was, for instance, the history of a lady. She was nameless, and she was responsible, in turn, for the history of a gentleman. The lady never got as far as that lane; but the gentleman we often saw there on those Sunday evenings, and his first words and sometimes all his words would be of her. How was she? Was she better? Ah, middlin', was she, middlin'? Ah dear, dear. He knew it. Felt it. What were we giving her? And he would stand there in some attitude of obese concern, pensive, mopping his half-bald head and light almost straw-coloured hair with his great crimson-and-white spotted handkerchief if it was very hot, his gestures melancholic, his voice paralysed at last by concern and reflection to the utterance of nothing but a single "Ah!" repeated in all shades of

meaning from doubt to hope, from hope to despair. And all for that lady.

It was the same in winter. He often came to see us then. Although he was a very large man, weighing anything from fourteen to sixteen stone or from ten to twelve score if weighed as they weigh pigs, he had very short legs, and they sagged spongily up and down with a regular motion in his wide trousers as he walked, as though he were doing a heavy dance to the tune played by his large brown boots, which let out prolonged dry squeaks at every step he took.

My grandmother at that time was a sufferer from asthma, a devilish complaint which often sent her to bed very early on winter evenings, so that my grandfather and I would often be alone downstairs, playing a game of dominoes and roasting potatoes under the fire and eating the hot potatoes as we played, when Quintus arrived. He would come up the garden path with the slow sedateness of a man squeaking down a church-aisle, he would knock heavily on the door, open it a crack and call "Anybody about?" and then come in, sitting on the chair nearest the door as though he were an unbidden guest. He would then take that large red-and-white spotted handkerchief from his behind-pocket, re-move his bowler-hat and proceed to wipe the sweat from his vast wurzel face, breathing in powerful spasmodic gasps as he did so.

Finally when he was at rest he would replace the handkerchief in his behind-pocket, lean back in his chair, gaze at my grandfather with a kind of melancholy expectation, and in a profound bass ask that eternal question:

"Well, boss, how is she?"

He had a perpetual habit of referring to my grandfather as boss, though they had been friends since boyhood. My grandfather would reply:

"She's easier, Quint, she's easier."

"Ah?"

"A lot easier."

"Ah? She worrit me, boss, she worrit me."

"She worrit me. But she's easier, a lot easier."

"Last Sunday," Quintus would say, "I couldn't forgit her. I couldn't git her out o' me mind. Does she eat anything?"

"Eats like a thacker."

"Ah! That's better beer. That's more like it."

They would use words of wonder and relief delivered with extreme earnestness, and finally there would be a long silence between them, a silence as though of blessed thankfulness.

It took me, a small boy, a very long time to realise that this conversation and the portentous silence which followed it did not concern my grandmother and her almost perpetual sufferings from asthma. It did not occur to me until the conversations became less secretive that it concerned not her and her sufferings but my grandfather's prize sow and her pregnancy.

"When," Quintus would say, "d'ye count she'll come due?"

"I count about next Thursday."

"By God, she's a good gal!" Quintus would burst out suddenly. "God A'mighty, she's a good gal!"

This sow was, in fact, for Quintus and my grandfather, the wonder of all the world. I do not know, now, how many times she conceived and brought forth, but it was an astounding number. But what was most astonishing was not the number of her conceptions but the number of pigs in each of her litters. She had

begun by modestly bringing forth ten or twelve and then gradually, with maturity and practice, had delivered fourteen or fif-
teen, and then sixteen, twice, and then seventeen, twice, and then
eighteen, and then to the colossal jubilation of Quintus and my
grandfather there came a time when she delivered nineteen.

Finally there was a period of almost drunken speculation when
my grandfather and Quintus hoped that, by the Grace of God, she
would deliver twenty. They spoke of her for many weeks with an
almost ecstatic tenderness, leaning over her sty-rails to scratch her
scaled back, affectionately smooth her hoary bristles and gaze into
her pink eyes with a kind of expectant rapture. If she were to have
twenty, God A'mighty, if she were to have twenty! If they had
been religious men at all I believe they would have prayed for that
prodigious delivery.

But it never happened. She was finished. She brought forth
what seemed to Quintus and my grandfather a paltry litter of ten or
twelve, and finally they had her slaughtered.

At the time of the cutting up of the carcass Quintus was a
frequent visitor. No longer able to ask after the welfare of the sow,
he would sit there and discuss with affection and enthusiasm the

promise of her bacon and sample the taste of her once noble and now collared head. She seemed to him as admirable in death as she had been in life. Had my grandfather a mite o' liver to spare, or a jowl, or a taste o' the chitterlings? It was as though he wanted these things as a souvenir of her fruitfulness. Long afterwards, when the sow herself had become a kind of mythical wonder, I would see him, in some pause of the conversation, turn his mild fat face towards the kitchen ceiling, and his eyes would rest on the muslined hams and the bacon sides glistening with salt as though with a powder of fine diamonds, and an expression of reminiscent beatitude would come over his face, as though he were reflecting on her wonder and her charm and her mortality.

He worshipped her. Indeed, I believe he worshipped not only her, but the race of pigs in its entirety. It may be that my memory is poor, but I never remember him talking of anything but pigs —pigs and pig-keeping, sows and stores, litters and the promise of litters. It did not occur to me until long afterwards that, with his fat body and his mild fair-lashed eyes and sober fleshiness, he was rather like some charming old sow himself.

But I should wrong him very much if I seemed to suggest that he had no other affections. I have said that he came to see us most often in winter; in summer he had other and more delightful pursuits.

He would be engaged, very often on those summer evenings, down that quiet meadow-lane where there was no traffic, in taking his hens for their evening walk. Very slow and deliberate and dignified, he would walk down towards the river, and the three hens, like three small white dogs, would follow him, clucking with happiness. He would proceed, at great leisure, between those high honeysuckled hedges, as far as the river. And there he would pause and gaze at the water, the hens would gaze at the water too, and finally they would all return.

Sow and hens have long since gone, but Quintus remains. He has suffered a common Midland fate: he is a countryman living in a town. And when I see him sometimes as he proceeds with solemn deliberation through the streets of the Midland town in which he now lives, his large wooden swill-buckets heavy on his sway-tree, I marvel not that he is still alive or that he still keeps and worships pigs, but that he has not changed at all.

His face has become if anything more like an earthy beetroot than the mangel-wurzel I imagine it to have been, the tame white hens have been replaced by a small tame absurd white dog, and his hair is no longer so thick and no longer corn-coloured but white. Otherwise he seems to me not to have changed an atom from the figure I used to know.

And indeed if he had changed it would make no difference to me. I am inclined to think of him as an eternal figure: not as the countryman living in the town, nor even as the man who worships pigs, but as the man who expressed his love of living things by taking his hens for gentle and solemn constitutionals on the summer evenings of a quieter age.

Fish and Fishermen

So it took us hours, sometimes, to get to that river. And because it took us so long it seemed doubly good to arrive. After that crazy lane, baked hard by sun, with the heat kept close and suffocating by the vast hedges, it was a delicious relief to see, from the stone bridge, the quiet breadth of water. There is nothing so tranquillising as the sight of a piece of water. And standing on the bridge, gazing down into the depth of water with its caverns of sunlight and shade and its long hair strands of emerald weed, we lapsed into a momentary trance of restfulness.

The river there was not wide, thirty or forty feet perhaps. There are countries where it would not be a river at all. But to us it was not only *a* river, but *the* river. For me, as a boy, its fascination lay not so much in its breadth as in its depth, in its profound weed-grown darknesses. It had, here and there, the reputation of being bottomless, and to me, standing above, trying to fathom it with my eyes, it looked it. A great sand-coloured shelf protruded out from the bank and then, immediately, there was a drop that seemed to go down into the heart of the world. Yet the men of grandfather's and even my father's time had skated on it with comfort.

So for me that stream had not only a tranquillising effect, but a terrifying effect. It was a small terror, spasmodic: a sudden shoot of terror up the spine. But then, hadn't I been brought up in terror of it? Hadn't it been dinned and thundered into me never to go near that stream? If I went too near, did I know it would draw me, like a magnet, and drag me in and drown? Did I want to go into the bury-hole?

Yet it fascinated me, in that subtle, powerful way that water does fascinate. In any landscape with water it is the water that catches the eye and holds it and draws it back with some kind of magnetism again and again. The river held my eyes in the same way. It hypnotised me. If it were not the near water, it was the middle distance, where downstream the river forked for the mill back-water, or the far distance, where a greater and older bridge made a stone skyline and shut out the miles of meadows beyond. I was held by the texture and flow of it, by that oily glassiness that falls on water after a hot day, by its brilliance or its almost golden colour after rain, by the spin and ripple and strength of the current moving like great muscles, by the twist and play of it about a reed-flag, by the rise of a fish breaking the surface with great expanding wheels, by the flick and dance of mayflies making their own miniature pin-wheels, by the flap and plop of the small water-waves against the bank or the bridge stones, by endless swaying and swooning motions of those tresses of water-weed, and finally and most constantly by the perpetual implacability and power of it as it flowed on and on.

This is a sensation that you never get with a brook. It is peculiar to rivers. With a brook there is no sense of strength, or implacability, or terror. There is a feeling almost of cheekiness, of flippancy. With a river there is a concentration, a maturity. It is a force. It is not merely a volume of water travelling on a set course from one point to another. It has become a living thing, with its own defined and complex character, its own idiosyncrasies and with something very like its own soul.

And yet, the moment we came down off that bridge and set foot on firm land, on the stream's own level, and felt the grass under our feet, the river lost all its terrors and much of its sense of implacable power. It became simply a piece of quiet water flowing easily down through quiet meadows. We were nearer to it, and yet, in some way, removed. We saw it from a new and more comforting angle. We looked across and along it, no longer down.

And, in the falling late summer evening light, it looked enchanting. Having come down by one lane, we always went back, if possible, by another. That meant a journey, along the tow-path, upstream, from one bridge to another. Making that journey was a great joy. All over the flat meadows the hay would be thick for cutting or cut for carrying, the sweetness of mown grass and buttercup and moon-daisy and clover something that we drank in, in great tangible draughts of intoxication. The fish would be rising, men would still be fishing. Lovers would be walking in sturdy arm-round-waist fashion or lying in the hay or propping up the tow-path gates. The light would be falling, the river losing its colour, the day losing its heat. We heard the tiny shrillings of bats and swallows, the cluck of moorhens and, very rarely, the strange almost crude cry of corncrakes, a sudden mysterious croak from across the marsh followed by the queerest of silences. It was all very peaceful, very idyllic, a scene put to sleep by its own combination of quiet sound and quiet colour and the quiet sunlight on its unpretentious horizons.

Then, half a mile farther on, it came to life again. We reached the wharf and the pub, or rather a house that had been a pub. It stood square and solid, of grey stone with a reddish roof of tiles, at the top of a small rise. From its front door a sort of wide yard sloped down to what had been, in the old days, a landing wharf. Then the place had been a curious combination of pleasure and commerce, a pub and a wharf in one. I often think of the clash of that life: of bargees and women, fights, drunkenness, jealousy, boasting, debauchery, argument, of all sorts of emotional and hectic and even animal conflict. Nor are these mere conjectures of my own, mere fancies of what the life there might have been like. I heard, over and over again, and drank in, greedily, tales of hearsay that left no doubt as to what that life had been like in the years before the end of the century. And what I didn't hear, I guessed at, as children do, putting two and two together and making always five. I heard funny stories, cranky stories, shady stories, incredible stories, bits of tragedy, odd events that had become, as they do in country places, local legends, the original tale lost in the huge bundle of impossibility that time had heaped on it. I heard that wonderful story of boastfulness, of how two men, fully liquored, had boasted and wagered one hot Sunday evening of how well they could dive from the height of the hunchback bridge, and of how finally it came to not only how well they could dive but how well they could swim, and then to how long they could stay under. They undressed and the crowd, big always on fine Sunday evenings, got excited and laid bets and gathered down at the water's edge. The men dived, and disappeared and after a moment or two one man came up. It was clear that he had lost, but it was not clear for some time, for a long time, by how much he had lost and by how much the other had won. Then it became clear, subsequently, that the other had won by an infinite margin. He never came up at all. It was only one story of many, one small fragment in the rough and rich history of that dingy house with its decaying bit of waterfront.

Years later I was to write a novel about that house and to be blamed, of course, here and there, for overdrawing things. Remembering what I had heard and knowing what I did know, I could only reply that, if there were faults, they were on the other side. It was almost impossible to overdraw that life. Still worse, it was impossible to draw it accurately. My only chance was in understatement. And now, when I think of it, it must have taken me an unconscionable time to write that book. I must have begun it, getting the focus, the colour, the incidentals, the breath of it, the skeleton, twenty years ago, standing on that small bridge, looking downstream, over the hay-cocked meadows, towards the sea.

But we never met, though I always hoped we should meet, the one man I longed to meet on or near that river—the queer sepulchral figure of my father's own uncle, a great tall black bird of a man, sombre, solitary, almost mystic in his air of removal from life, an almost legendary figure, the most divine exponent of piscatorial art who ever fished, perhaps, in those waters. Rook was a master. He was gifted with that blessed faculty that is perhaps, after all, the sum total of genius—second sight. He could see where other men were blind. He fished where other men merely angled. He caught where others hoped. It was said of him, and said by

other fishermen, that he could go to that river, any day, in season, and fish in its barrenest reaches and haul out pounders with the maddening simplicity of a man doing a conjuring trick. He lived by fishing. He gave lessons. He was the local *maestro*. And it is my one huge regret in life and my one real grudge against my father that I was never allowed to learn at his feet. My father should have gone to him and said, "Rook, Uncle, this is my beloved son, in whom I am well pleased. Teach him all you know. Make him a fisherman worthy of the family." But he didn't, and there it is. Blessed with an ancestor like Rook, all I can do is to catch gudgeon.

For that reason, perhaps, I have the tenderest feelings towards all fishermen. If they are skilful and lucky I envy them, if they are, like myself, bunglers and unlucky into the bargain, I admire their patience, their infinite capacity for hope, their almost touching determination. There is nothing ferocious about a fisherman. His art demands of him that he shall be gentle, soft, quiet, self-effacing. A butterfly-hunter can exhibit more lust, more joy in the chase. And he also has, at least, the consolation of pursuing something he can see. But not the fisherman. Poor wretch, he is not only hunting something which he cannot see but something which very often isn't there. In hunting you are sorry, if you are sorry at all, for the quarry, in shooting for the bird, but in fishing you have no such feelings for the fish. They are for the fisherman. He is the one kind of hunter who starts, and continues, at a disadvantage. Fox-hunting angers me largely because of the colossal unfairness of the odds. One hundred and fifty creatures against one! Why not, pray, one man, one horse, one dog, one fox? In shooting, the velocity of the bullet so far exceeds the velocity of the bird as to give the shooter the same fatalistic advantage as if he were to seize a beer-barrel in order to crush a beetle. But the poor fisherman —with that one rod, with its one line, its one hook, one worm, one fly, he pits himself against a creature of another element, of the subtlest and most mysterious of worlds. If a hunter runs his fox to earth he can dig him out. But if a fisherman loses his fish how can he bail out the whole of the waters that hide it? How can he even follow it? How can he even know what it was? What size it was? What breed? Roach or gudgeon or tench or chubb or perch? He is done like a dinner. He is setting his art and reason, his skill with the most primitive of tackle, against the sublime artfulness of Nature. He is setting himself, huge, clumsy, painfully immobile, against an unseen creature of supreme swiftness and magical mobility. There is something almost eternal and ageless about it. It is the most primitive of sports, unchanged in its essentials by the passage of time or scientific revolution or the habits of man. Wherever there is a piece of water deep enough for the drowning of a cat you will find men or boys dangling lines in it with the same immobile hope and comic expectation as men did, far back, on the shores of Tiber or Ganges or Galilee.

Fishermen have only one fault, and we may pardon it. Their deviation into hyperbole is, after all, often their only consolation. Also, they may have been right. Any lost fish may have been colossal. Pike have been caught up to seventy pounds. Which reminds me, now, of the postcard sent to me by a lady, an earnest creature interested in the arts, the antiquities and what not of gastronomy, in particular the gastronomy of old England, and in special particular fishing gastronomy. Would I, a countryman, as one interested in such things, tell her how many pike per head she needed for a small dinner party?

All fishermen are childish. Hence that universal passion for exaggeration. In that they differ from all other hunters. You never see a sportsman hastening home, after a pheasant shoot, with that look of seraphic jubilation on his face that you see on the faces of fishermen. You never see him leap about, in smoke-rooms, spreading out his hands assuring you that but for the Grace of God and bad luck he would have shot a pheasant with the wing-span of

an eagle. You never hear a huntsman boast of a fox as big as a
leopard. Yet ever since there were fishermen men have gone home
to their wives or their friends and even, I suppose, to their
mistresses, to tell, with that charming air of comic jubilation, of
mythical fish beyond the bounds of all imagination but their own.

In that way, from listening to stories, I grew up to suppose that
my grandfather was no mean fisherman. Hadn't he caught eels by
the ton, jack with snares of wire, trout of arm's length? And then,
once, in casual fashion, I mentioned this to an old contemporary of
his. Fish? He met me with cracking laughter. Fish? He would tell
what kind of fisherman my grandfather was. He could, in the first
place, never catch a tiddler. Look, it was he, the contemporary, did
I understand, who caught everything. George never had a bite. He
would fish all day without a bite. But the desperate thing about it
was that, somehow, by hook or crook or stealing or something, he
had to take home something in the shape of a fish or else be done
for. How else prove that he had been fishing? No fish, no fishing.
And if no fishing, what? Where had he been? To the pub? With a
lady? Acting the fool? Up to no good? A bit of a Tartar at times,
my grandmother would want things straight. Oh, yes! Therefore,
before he dare go home, my grandfather would humbly beg the
favour of a gudgeon, or a roach, or a little eel. A gudgeon! That's
the sort of fisherman he was, this man cried in triumph. A man
who had to beg a gudgeon before he dare go home!

But I will not have it, and I must vindicate him. Years after those
Sunday evening excursions we went one day, my grandfather and
brother and I, to fish under one of the large grey willows that lined
the bank between one bridge and another. It was an afternoon of
staggering heat, the water lay like hot glass, and what fish we

expected to catch under that arid sky I don't know. My brother and I sat in a sweat of boredom and my grandfather sat hunched up with the meditative somnolence of the old. The floats lay and mocked us.

Suddenly my grandfather let out a stupendous yell, staggered to his feet, did a series of crazy circumlocutions and bawled for help. We rushed up, supposing he was being pulled in. Just at this moment he executed a magnificent flourish, strained like a man in some herculean contest of strength, and landed a four-foot eel—a three-foot eel. Time, like distance, lends enchantment, and it is difficult to be exact. Perhaps it was a two-foot-six eel. But you have my word that it seemed to us, bored and stabbed by heat, colossal.

We bore it home in triumph, reed strung through head, carrying it in turns. What a catch! What fishermen! We got ready to show it to all we should meet. We got ready to explain it, exhibit it, pass it off, discuss it. Here was no mythical fish, but something tangible, measurable. A great catch. We prepared to accept congratulations, to be objects of envy to all we should see.

And all up that meadow lane where, on those summer Sunday evenings of the past we had met scores of men, we never met a soul.

The Flood

Suddenly, generally in winter, occasionally in summer, that valley underwent a wholesale and fascinating transformation. It was a transformation not only in appearance, but atmosphere. From being pastoral, it became wild; from being idyllic, it became desolate. You went to bed, one night, with the rain deluging down on a world of sepulchral blackness, to wake up, next morning, like some minor Noah, to be confronted by a world in flood. You could look down, suddenly, on a vast ice-coloured lake stretching for twenty miles upstream to eighty miles downstream, almost from the source to the coast. You were living, all at once, on the shores of an inland sea.

Though to us, standing well above it, it looked less like a sea than some colossal river two miles wide, a vast white and, in some way, cold and savage waterway. It was as though the whole nature of the real and now pathetic river itself had been changed, over-night, by a cataclysm. It was as though the Nene had been turned into the Rhine. Water would be pouring down, everywhere, throughout the whole width of the valley, three feet deep, rising, perhaps to five feet deep, submerging hedges, lapping up against the roadways, beating and flopping in sudden wind-caught waves above the arches of bridges. It was a great wild wateriness, a desolation broken by the shipwrecks of haystacks and cow-hovels, by bare willows leaning over as though being forced over by the great weight of water, by isolated islands of grass, by some occasional drifting boat, by a barge stranded in the stream like a small inglorious ark with galley chimneys gustily smoking.

It was a time of some excitement, naturally. "The floods are out! Did you know?" We took walks to see it all. We stood on the high valley side, above it, and looked down on the receding miles and miles of water extending far down towards the sea, and watched and marvelled. If it were windy, with a little sun, we saw it broken up and transformed by motion and light from a vast iron-coloured piece of water to a shining and dancing lake. So agitated, winking silver, never still, it looked unreal. It looked once again idyllic and in some way impermanent. Then that look of delicate imper-manency used to make me wish, at once, that it were permanent, that it would remain there for the rest of time, a great elongated lake in which we could watch, every day, the delicate or savage or stormy or placid reflections of changing light or, by night, the moon and stars, the floating lantern chains of street lights and the solitary window-lights of isolated farm-houses in the black acres of valley beyond the towns.

For at night we got, more than ever, the impression of living on the edge of a lake. Darkness blotted out all that remained of hedges and haystacks and land, and the water lay in what seemed to be a great sheet of glassy blackness. At dusk, lights from the opposite side of the valley began as it were to spill down on it and float there, like golden blots of liquid themselves, darkness increasing them, until finally on full clear nights of proper winter blackness the whole valley was floating with lights as though with a fantastic fleet of lanterned boats, as in a Chinese harbour. It all belonged to a world of unreality.

For the reality of it, the right feeling, for the true atmosphere and taste of the thing, we had, as usual, to get close to it. It was all very well to stand, high up, away from it, and see it all as some oriental harbour of fairy lights and cheat ourselves into a belief of its reality, but for the true atmosphere, the atmosphere of watery space and solitude and grey desolation, we had to go down and stand on the small stone-and-brick bridge, by the now pathetically small pub, and look down to sea again.

Then we got the width and strength of it: the immense space of water, the great power of it. There, at a point where in summer boys bathed and paddled and men stood up to their thighs to wash sheep, the river came under the bridge in a great curdled torrent, crazily rapid, a chaotic maelstrom of cross-currents and whirl-pools, washing and spewing over the rotten wharf, drowning small trees, swirling thickly and powerfully out across the meadows like a yellow current in the otherwise placid space of water. It was hard to believe it was the same river. It was now not only powerful, but it seemed omnipotent. In England, in a country where, generally speaking, the landscape is well-behaved, a tor-rent like this seemed out of place. Tearing down, breaking its banks, doing its vast transformation act of turning the world to water, it upset all proportions and perspectives. It made the small stone pub standing precariously on its bank seem as fragile as an upturned boat of cardboard; it turned the willows into nothing but the skeletons of torn-out umbrellas; it gave the few black still unsubmerged bits of hedgerow the likeness of nothing but scraps of horse-dung. Most of all, it made the memory of itself ridiculous.

Standing there, looking over acres and acres of water, I used to come to a better understanding of our friend Noah. I used to magnify that small flood and spread it over the whole county, the whole of England, the world, until Noah, I decided, was the victim of unduly harsh circumstances. The ways of God, as depicted in the Old Testament, are so magnificently wholesale. Not enough to flood Palestine, not even enough to flood Arabia; it must be the whole world. Poor Noah! The sight of the Nene valley, two miles wide, five feet deep, with its wrecks of hovels and haystacks, was enough to convince me what a comfort a bird can be.

It was the birds, in fact, which revolutionised that whole piece of water. Suddenly, from nowhere, as quickly and magically as the floods themselves, they appeared in thousands. The greater the floods, the wilder the weather, the more birds came down on these waters. It was as though they had become monstrously rich in fish. Gulls came down in such great wild flocks that sometimes, when they settled and were still and then rose abruptly, it seemed as if the water took momentary wings. Great congregations of peewits followed, mingling with them on unsubmerged places or careering high above. I am not sure that the peewit, whether paired or gathered in its winter congregations, is not the best of all English larger birds. It behaves with extraordinary grace and volatility, careering, diving, planing, swooping, stunting, performing its decoy trick of despair and terror with such acrobatic passion that, often, it defeats itself. There is something just a fraction too expert about that performance. But it is, even so, fascinating, almost terrifying. Then they look charming, too, at rest: very erect and aristocratic, with their perky cockatoo cockades. But gathered in those vast winter companies, above and about the floods, they ceased almost to be birds, at least individual birds. They would marshal, sometimes, high up and begin to go through a prolonged series of strange manœuvres, beautifully ordered but somehow crazy, as though they were the victims of a kind of military madness. I have seen them go up and round and over and up and round and down and up again with such beautifully drilled precision, flashing alternate black and white of wings against the blue winter sky, that it seemed uncanny. They seemed to be gathering and manœuvring for some colossal celestial parade. And I can think of no other bird which, in England, behaves like that. Rooks and jackdaws go through fantastic exhibitions of what is either sheer joy or terror at times of high wind and at the approach of storm and rain; but there is no order in them. They behave with individual craziness, turning, leaping up, riding on sudden wind-currents, falling as though with wounded wings, and it is an astonishing performance. But it has no order, none of that beautiful perfectly timed modulation of the peewit flocks wheeling with the precision of trained pigeons.

Gulls and peewits would mingle freely on the green flood islands and occasionally rooks would join them, not in great numbers, but as though out of curiosity. Moorhens would struggle fussily about

and always, of course, the tame ducks, serene, unperturbed, seraphically white and comic. Then we got stray herons and heronshaw, aloof and solitary, and some wild duck in not very great numbers, and very rarely some wheezing and honking strings of wild geese flying across the waters with powerful haste. But the really amazing arrivals were the swans.

They arrived in scores and even hundreds. They seemed to have deserted every baronial lake and swannery in England, as though overjoyed at the chance of exchanging, even briefly, their own tame and sheltered waters for these vast wild floods. They ranged from strings of half a dozen to great companies of twenty or thirty or more. They rode in serene possession, snow-white, except, of course, the cygnets, intensely majestic, superbly arrogant. They fed voraciously, plunging in flood-bottoms with comic hidden necks. They disported themselves with that peculiar and fitting dignity with which swans occasionally express their light-heartedness: wheeling archly round, letting the wind steer them into some sudden but essentially decent waltz, half unfolding their wings, quivering them stiffly, bringing them back to serene rest again. The cobs would engage in small feats of masculine swank, rushing at each other in starts of anger, breasting the water in fierce gestures, free-wheeling, surveying the world with the defiance of pure lordliness. So white and graceful, with their air of immense latent strength, they were continually attractive.

The swan, in its natural element, of course, and not on land, always seems to me the angel among English larger birds. The peacock is more brilliant, but not prouder. It has something effeminate about it, something a little oriental. It is fussed and fussy. Heron and eagle and goose and buzzard all have characteristics, of solitariness or savagery, of clumsiness or rarity, which spoil their chances of competition. But in grace, strength, accessibility, friendliness, perfection of colouring and supreme beauty, the swan scores every time. It is the absolute lord among birds. Long association with man has made it almost an emblem, and yet has not tamed it. And in these floods of ours, on the grey acres of water under the wintry skies, it was in its element. It had space, background. It gave them a final touch of permanency. Its air of superb tradition was transposed to the waters themselves, until it seemed as though both swans and floods had been there for ever.

The Frost

All these things, swans, peewits, gulls, the sight of the floods themselves, were more or less minor excitements. Except for the birds and some occasional wanderer, like myself, the valley would be deserted. Nobody got into a state of active excitement; floods were a phenomenal event, but we were used to them. Again, the only enjoyment they would give us was æsthetic. It never occurred to anybody to use them for physical pleasures, for winter swimming matches, for instance, or regattas. The most we could do was to stand on the bridges and by the mills and stare and marvel at the great spread and power of water.

But then, if we were in luck, something happened. The air changed, the days cleared, and the feeling of wet south-west humidity was suddenly driven out. The days were crisp and we watched an almost crackling brilliance of stars at night. And then, suddenly, the mornings had the bitterness of frost on them.

Then we did get excited. All that water—and frost! The sudden harshness of the days, the black temper of frost, was exhilarating. All we needed, we knew, on those shallow flood waters, were three successive nights of tolerable freezing, of really quiet deadly frost, and then we skated.

I should be happier if it were freezing now, as I write. The land, everywhere, suffers from an intolerable spongy humidity, from an excess of sultry autumn rain that weighs down on the spirit. Gales of unsleeping savagery have lashed us one day from the south and south-west, the next from north and north-east, as though in spite. The land has the dejected look of a drenched animal. The woods are torn to shreds. Ploughed fields, with corn already spiking up a bright emerald, have the wretched winter lifelessness on them. The gales leap across the hills with a roar, ripping out the last shreds of autumn overnight. Rain comes in prolonged relentless periods and we see nothing from it but, all about us, the sodden mess of the land.

Now in a river country, in a valley, you would see something for your money. You would see the river perform the trick of increasing its size a hundredfold: the only object, in a whole landscape, capable of performing such a feat in such a time. A wood, once grown, remains fixed and moulded; nothing can suddenly provoke it into any kind of manifold increase at all. It remains as fixed as a monument. Fields also remain fixed; they do not suddenly expand into vast celestial pastures. Hills, defying all the proverbial faith in the world, are not suddenly turned into mountains. The wind can roar with omnipotent and staggering savagery for a whole winter without materially changing the face of these things. It accomplishes no more than the breath of a flea on a candle-flame.

But a night and a day of rain will change a river into a sea. Better still, three nights of freezing will turn it into a paradise.

And that change has an extraordinary effect on the spirit. It clarifies it, makes it wonderfully light, almost abandoned. If you doubt this you should see the change in the temper of the Nene valley people when, after days of flood, the great expanses of water are suddenly frozen. Ice! Skating! The whole neighbourhood behaves with something of the excitement of small children.

For there is nothing at all, in the whole world of sport and pastime, so exhilarating as skating. It has every virtue that a sport should have, and no vices. It affords opportunities of skill, grace, perfect pleasure; it has just a pinch of the salt of danger in it; it asks for no teams, no clubs, no opposing sides, no petty competition, no snobbery of dress or behaviour. With a pair of skates a man can get as near to being a bird as he ever will without going up into the air: a divine feeling, easy, exhilarating, untiring. There is nothing better. When almost all sports have become commercialised or cheapened or even embittered by publicity, skating remains a perfectly friendly, social, beautiful thing, to be enjoyed for its own sake. It stands out at the other end of the scale from hunting, not seeking to hurt or pursue or terrify anything or anybody. It is democratic; class distinctions do not touch it. In fact it breaks down social barriers, so that there seems to be more friendliness and laughter on a stretch of ice than anywhere else in the world.

We used to rush down to the bridge by the wharf, skates ready, almost before the ice could, in all reason, be expected to bear. I have been first on that marsh, before the sun had any power at all, when the virgin ice with its light dusting of rime or snow had no mark on it except the starry prints of birds' feet and when great veining cracks split and shot out every step I took. But if it cracks it bears; if it bends it breaks. And sure enough, cracks mean nothing; it is that sickening undulating bending that is charged with danger.

I learned on an antique pair of my grandfather's skates, *circa* 1870, strap-on, long runners, screws eaten away by rust and corruption. The division of time spent on them and time spent on my backside was roughly equal. I got into all those crazy entanglements of the beginner: arms windmilling, skates up, bottom down, all those acrobatics which are part of the fun. And I would look with reverence and envy at very old men and even quite old women who had appeared out of retirement, with skates of even greater antiquity than my own, to skate again with all the elasticity and grace of youth. How do they do it? What is it, in skating, that enables a man to perform that trick of perpetual youth, of being able to skate on with agility into the years of his dotage? Imagine a man reappearing, at seventy, to astonish the younger generation at football. Yet always, on that ice, there would be men of sixty and seventy, hands behind backs, heads forward, bodies light, scissoring along as though on oiled limbs.

And there would be I, young and agile, struggling along as though on legs of lead, encountering all the difficulties and obstacles in the world: ice-bedded stones and sticks, tufts of sedge, other beginners. One by one the straps broke and then, at last, the skates broke. I rushed up to the blacksmith's, had them mended, and rushed back again. Straps held now by bits of string, bootlaces, safety-pins, and what not, I rushed on to the ice with renewed vigour and confidence, only to go bottom over head at once, as though by clockwork.

Then, in time, all that crazy perseverance was rewarded. I could skate. I could begin to travel with ease. I could look at the sky. I could even look, out of the corner of my eye, at the other beginners doing their own first acrobatics. I could feel that rare joy that only skating can give, the joy of extreme exhilaration, of travelling by a process that seems hardly to belong to earth.

Only then, of course, could I even begin to look at the world in which I moved: that still, taut winter world of profound coldness, with its sugar frost and sugared trees and sedges, the beautiful loftiness of the pale-blue wintry sky, the almost red winter sun falling very early across the meadows in the afternoons towards a horizon already smoky and tawny with the promise of frost. Once fairly expert, I could drink in the glitter and sparkle of the early morning world, when the ice is still like glass, black and clear, with the first skate marks on it like crescents and scribbles of chalk; and when, on the edge of the marsh, where sedge and rush make a big circle, the white cat-ice, thin as window-glass, waterless underneath, cracks off like brittle shot in the silent, frozen air. Sedges and grasses and reeds are then, in the early morning, fantastic. Frost embalms them and they stand rigidly like the sugared ghosts of themselves, relics of a strange ice-age. And in very severe, wicked weather, the first skin of ice would be forming a lip on the river edges, a jagged cream-coloured or blue-white line like the depth-line round a sea coast on a map, and the river itself would look in some way ominous, deadly smooth, as though beyond the cream and white ice another expanse of ice were flowing slowly down, like shining running jet.

Then as the day went on I could look at the people; I mean I could look them in the face. I could stand and talk with old friends and join in that peculiarly joyful laughter that you always get on ice: everybody laughing and shouting with great gaiety, girls shrieking, men shouting greetings, the whole combination of light sound flung up into the air from the ice as though from a soundboard of glass, and mingled with it the sound of skates, that thin musical cutting sound of steel on ice that, for many people, is a great joy.

Then, as the day went on and people thickened, some enterprising gent would arrive with a potato-oven or hot chestnuts or a tea-urn, and set up by the bridge; and you would skate over and warm hands by the fire and break a potato or two, or drink a cup of tea, and talk and laugh, and wave hands to friends and take great breaths of pleasure and feel, generally, that you could, if only there were ice, skate on and on and down to the sea.

And once, it seems, in the days when the climate of this island, like its manners and morals, was less disturbingly complex and more inclined to keep to its seasons, they did skate down to the sea. At least they skated for forty miles, all down river: under bridges, missing locks, by mills and wharves and villages and pubs, in a fabulous frost that lasted thirteen weeks, and then in another that lasted six. Colossal days! In England, where winters are often more like wet reflections of spring, it seems like a Russian fairy tale. Men put on their skates, then, by the fireside and skated off from their back doors and down those lanes where, later, I was to walk as a boy. Horses and carts were drawn across the ice; bonfires were lighted. Bonfires and hot potatoes and frozen rivers and Victorian maidens in muffs!—it was a miracle painted on a Christmas card.

But of all the curious miracles performed by frost I used to notice one, on that marsh, in particular. All the birds would disappear.

All that vast concourse of gulls and peewits and swans would vanish utterly. A few rooks, a few starlings flying over in the red afternoons, an occasional heron—nothing more remained. When did they go? By night? Or by day, warned by instinct of frost? Whenever they went, I never saw them. And how good it would have been to see them, the great grey uprising of gulls, the immense martialling of peewits, the glorious looming away of the swan cloud. But we never saw them go or, in fact, when the thaw began, return. They came and went on almost fabulous wings.

Birds on ice become, in fact, very curious. Swans behave with a kind of regal, fussy resentment. They understand that cruel transformation of their world from liquid to solid and they know what to do about it, but they are resentful in an archly pompous way that is quite comic. The old male tucks in his head and regards the ice and the world generally as a piece of presumptuous monstrosity. Paddling round, he keeps his special space of water moving and, if he is lucky, it never freezes. But he is always angry and now and then he breasts the water like a policeman pushing a crowd, sending up savage little waves that lap over the ice-rim. But most of all he is like some grave Canute, setting himself against the tide, keeping that circle of water free for himself and his mate, the very look of him keeping away all inferior intruders.

Those intruders will include, generally, coot and moorhen. Wild duck congregate alone, in great winter masses, and they seem quite happy on ice. They tone with a new skin of dark ice, on a lake, miraculously, their soft-shining feathers having, from a distance, very much that same dull bloom as the grey ice; so that suddenly, when they rise and tear up into the upper air with an almost snipe-swiftness, it seems for a moment as though the ice, like the floods at the rising of gulls, had taken wings. It is an impressive sight, a scattering of wild duck from ice, and it creates an impression of beautiful wildness and then of almost frantic terror as the ducks neck round and round in disorder before they can bring themselves to settle again.

But of all creatures on ice, coot are most comic. They behave like heavy-bottomed old ladies on the glass floor of a ballroom. They are hopeless and helpless. Alone, they can stand still or make short perilous careful excursions without much risk or comedy. But when danger comes they are startled into retreat. For some reason they do not fly. They elect to proceed by ice, and it is a procedure of absolute craziness. The coot flounders and flops and skates and hustles in something of the same dumb burlesque fashion as penguins. They wobble and stagger and their legs fly from under them exactly, in fact, as though they were trying to skate. It is all pathetically comic. Once out of danger, they rest on the ice with an utter lack of dignity but with a dazed look of immense relief at being able, at last, to stand more or less still.

They are more comic, indeed, than rooks, which is saying something. Rooks have an air of comicality that is wicked; they have an air of depraved reprobates. Even as I sit here, writing, a great crowd of rooks has just passed over, careering back to the rookery, with more fuss than a retreating army and for no apparent reason. They have come up from the river where, it is quite likely, something has frightened them very much. But for all their fear they look and sound like a flock of bird comedians. The main flock, jackdaws too, goes over with a great panic of cackling and squawking as though to warn the world of an impending typhoon. And then the wind is getting up, has increased its velocity con-

siderably even in the five minutes since they passed. It may be, then, not fear of man but fear of storm which has driven them. At any rate, they go over in a flight of serio-comic disorder. And they are followed, far behind, by a solitary rook who is the personification of all rooks and all rook comicality. Over he comes, bringing up the rear, a great bird cawing and cackling in fear and wrath as though he is a Jehovah among rooks, as though, after all, it is not man or storm but only he himself that is the terror. It is like some biblical enactment of divine anger, of an awful rook-god descending with a loud voice on an offending people. All that spoils it is that it is so funny. It is as though God were to have appeared and chastised the Israelites with an irate umbrella.

But rooks have an astonishing artfulness too; which is why, perhaps, that distant uncle of my father's, the master fisherman, was called that. Rook for cunning. All of which reminds me of all the shooting in which I ever took part in my life. We had a gun which we kept in a tool-barn; it hung among rat-traps and hoes and dibbers and snares and old horseshoes and tins of corn-cure and sickles and whetstones and what not. It was a muzzle-loader, a very ancient firearm that maybe had seen service in the Crimea or Waterloo or some earlier battle—who knows? It was a romantic gun for this reason and also for another reason. It took about a day to load it. So that whenever it rained torrentially and the land was neck-deep in mud, we sat there in the tool-barn and had a day loading the gun. This also served a double purpose; we not only loaded the gun but we cleared up all the rubbish. You could load the gun with anything; so we more or less swept up the place and rammed everything into the gun. We put in a little powder, of course, and then shot of various grades up to the size of wren's egg more or less, and then we rammed in all the swept-up bits of string, rats' nests, old nails, brace-buttons, screws, tin-tacks, bits of dried mice and in fact anything that would ram down and which, in course of time, would give some old rook something better to think about than new young beans and corn.

But somehow there were never any rooks about when we were loading the gun; the wheat lay birdless and untouched. There was therefore nothing to do but hang the gun up again, and wait for another day. This we did. In due course, when one morning we woke up to see the wheat covered with a black plague of rook wings, we got into a state of panic. My grandfather seized the gun, told me to keep back and set off across the field with the furtive bandy-leggedness of a man stalking prey. Crouching lower and lower, with the idea no doubt of making himself invisible, he got to within a furlong or two of the rooks and then stopped and, with a gesture of triumph, raised the gun to his shoulder. But before he could get a sight, the rooks were flying and cackling over the next parish.

So he had to turn round and come back and, reluctantly, hang up the gun again. No sooner had he hung it up than the wheat was black as a pall with rooks again. So down came the gun, off went my grandfather, and up went the rooks. All this happened again and again. He never got near enough to take a shot. Often it went on for weeks and weeks, until finally he was afraid to take a shot. There was some chance, it seemed, after this long time, of the gun shooting out of the wrong end: an unpleasant contingency, and one which we were anxious to avoid if possible. Only one course was therefore open to us: to fire off the gun from a distance.

And so at last we tied the gun to the pigsty rails with many lashings of rope, and then tied fifty yards of string to the trigger. Then we retreated. There would be an interval of almost painful silence, with the pigs in a state of pig-eyed apprehension, and then my grandfather pulled the string. The effect was terrific, volcanic. With a vast roar the charge went up and came down again on pigs and pigsties with the clatter of a bombardment: shot, nails, rats' nests, newspapers, brace-buttons, dried mice were scattered all over us like rain. And all the pigs tore hither and thither and squealed and bunted the sty-rails and moaned and grunted for hours afterwards.

This kind of shooting, the comic, as it were the Pickwickian, is all that I can enjoy. What we call ordinary shooting, that is of birds or men, I find too serious, altogether too highly charged. Compared with such a thing as skating—but the two are not comparable. Shooting is serious, vindictive, graceless, and hot and bloody business. Skating is superlatively graceful, gay, friendly—but I have already set out its delights and virtues.

All, that is, except one: which is skating in fog. One year, in the afternoon of Christmas Eve, a fog gathered and came down on the marsh of the Nene as we were skating there. It was a strange and weird experience. It was like skating in a world of ghosts. We lost ourselves and our friends. We skated almost on the edge of the river without knowing it. The echoes of skates and laughter were uncannily magnified and at the marsh-edge, where we so often found ourselves in ghostly bewilderment, the frost-bearded grasses and sedges were like strange ferns in some phantom ice-age.

The Second River

The Nene was an all-the-year-round river; we saw it in all its moods, in flood and drought, in frost and heat, and we felt very close to it. But the Ouse was a summer river; we never went to it except on the summery crest of the year; we never saw it in frost or flood or tempest or in anything like a mood of wildness at all. It was a purely idyllic stream.

At the point where I know them best, these two rivers run almost parallel, about ten miles apart, with the boundaries of their own counties forming a half-way line between them. Farther north from the Nene, about thirty miles, goes another parallel, the Welland. These three great rivers make as it were a great trident forking all across the pastures of the eastern Midlands. The handle of that trident is the Wash and these three pronged bits of water mark out, as sharply as though they were really colossal divisions of steel, three extraordinary separate and definite provinces of the English countryside. Beyond the Welland, the North begins: the stone walls, the big scabs of industry, the higher and sharper speech, the cocksureness of character. Between Welland and Nene runs a thin and separated tongue of the Midlands, neither one thing nor the other, neither north nor south, neither industrial nor agricultural: a country of ugly and bastard speech, of stout independence, of stone and pasture; of scabby jumped-up chapel-cum-villa towns, only fifty years ago one-street villages, lying side by side with some of the loveliest mansions of stone in these islands. The Nene reflects all of that jumbled complexity of character as though it were a mirror held and tilted through centuries by time and circumstance. It has all the characteristics of the country through which it flows; its valleys are pasture, its bridges stone; it has in certain places a drabness, almost a meanness, exactly like that of the towns past which it flows, as though time had washed the muck of them down to it; and then, above all, it is—or was—a navigated waterway, with tow-paths and locks and a certain dirty severity about it, without frills or humbug, a river with a purpose. Its left bank, looking towards the sea, is shorn for miles of all trees; long years of necessity—though there is never a barge except an old dredger goes down it now from one year's end to another —years of commercial necessity, have left it as bare as the tow-path of the canal. In a way, indeed, it is a canal, a canal with just enough independence to prevent it going as straight as an iron rule from source to sea. It wriggles, just north of my country, with a sudden sharp but controlled impetuosity. On the map it looks like a gesture of impatience, the sudden flip of someone anxious to get on. Yet this snakiness is a line drawn by an architect in comparison with the crazy behaviour of the Ouse through the countryside where I know it best. It turns and twists and doubles back on itself and changes its mind exactly like a woman under the stress of some extreme excitement. The difference between the Nene and the

Ouse is, in fact, the difference between masculine and feminine. The Nene is a straight and bony stream, utilitarian, unfrilled, not much to look at; the Ouse has a sort of womanliness about it, soft, indecisive, very beautiful, a broad bosom of a stream flowing through a country in which the very names of the villages are names coined by a soft-spoken and almost feminine people.

These villages form, in fact, one of the prime differences between Ouse and Nene. Centuries of extensive flooding, combined with reason, forced the Nene folk to build high up out of the valley; so that their villages—now so often industrialised towns—are perched up on the escarpment, in bare bleak situations without romance but, as it so happens, with ample room for expansion. So that villages built down on the very lip of the Nene are not common. This is exactly typical of the Nene mentality: use before prettiness, reason before romance. Thus the Nene has few lovely riverside towns, such as, for instance, Henley or Stratford or Bedford or Tewkesbury, but in compensation its people never get their feet wet. When the valleys of the Thames and the Medway flood and drive their inhabitants up to sleep on the roofs, I know that, except for an odd farmer who has forgotten his bullocks, nobody on the Nene is worrying much. The towns sit comfortably and unprettily out of danger.

But on the Ouse things are exactly reversed. For some reason, not because the river does not overflow its banks, the Ouse folk took no notice at all of, in my grandfather's words, the lessons of Nature, and their towns and villages are built on the stream. The result is a long chain of charming towns and villages whose names are exactly appropriate to such a soft-spoken and in a way soft-thinking people: Pavenham, Turvey, Olney, Stevington,

Harrold, Odell; Ely, Earith, Huntingdon, St. Neots, St. Ives. They are milky, dreamy names, names that sound like the evolutions of a people who were not properly awake—which, as I shall show in a moment, is still one of their prime characteristics. They are a people not only half asleep, but still in servitude.

All of these places by the Ouse are as lovely as their names, but the descendants of those who made them now pay for it dearly. Not only are they not healthy, which may account for that peculiar Bedfordshire sleepiness, but in times of flood there arises the question, very often, of getting the boats out. All along the roads by the Ouse you will see wooden bridges running along the hedge-sides; they are built up on four-foot stilts and, in summer, they seem superfluous. But in winter they are very essential ways of escape. The people must then be in a quandary: whether it is better to live in ugliness and be dry, or whether it is better to live in beauty and be marooned.

But, on consideration, I wonder very much if, after all, they ponder that. Industry smashes many things, and in the Nene valley it not only smashed all the universal and usual things like peace and quiet and ideals and modes of life, but it smashed, absolutely and I hope for ever, the feudal servitude of man to master. But in the Ouse valley there is no industry, and the ghost of that feudal servitude survives. The people, having nothing else to give them life, are still in bondage to the land, which means that they are still in bondage to those who own the land. They are a people who have not gained emancipation. True, they have not been jockeyed, like the Nene folk, from one hobby-horse to another, from the man-master to the machine-master, from feudalism to industrialism. But they have not had their revolution. They remain very rural, staunchly and stupidly clinging to a belief in that now almost bankrupt illusion, the Victorian squirearchy.

You may hear the accent of this almost pathetic faith, which amounts in a way to idolatry, in the speech of the Ouse folk. They speak with a pseudo-cultured accent, something midway between the genteel and the cockney, aping the gentry, speaking with a sort of ever-so-niceness, a careful too-niceness, as though you, the listener, might by chance belong to the gentility too. And generally their standards are genteel too. How, indeed, can they help it? They are completely surrounded by gentility in the shape of retired captains, seedy lords, real shabby gentry clinging to their absurd mansions and in some cases letting them off into flats; by hunting people, by doubtful Honourables, by here and there some vague cultured authoress still writing novels in the grand manner and paying for them to be published. There is no industry: on these people and on the land the Ouse folk are dependent for life. It is not surprising therefore that they grow up, not only with an almost fearful regard for the life they serve, but with an unconscious desire to emulate it. It is the same in many purely rural places, places to which the industrial revolution has still really not penetrated. So almost wherever you go in the Ouse valley you will hear that accent of pseudo-gentility, the accent of people struggling hard not only to keep up genteel appearances but to show the world that they are really a little better than they seem to be.

I remember one such woman, dead now. We called on her, a friend and myself, to negotiate for the purchase of the house she lived in. It was a square stone house overlooking the Ouse itself, and has long since been pulled down: a damp-green neglected place with wild orchard and funereal Irish yews and long-disused stables. A circle of great walnut trees kept out light and air, and the apples in the orchard squashed in the wet September grass as we walked. The place had not only an air of decay about it, but an air of genteel decay.

And when we knocked at the door the woman who came was the personification of the house: thin and nice-lipped, with the brooch of respect pinned high on her skinny throat, her hands bony and well-bred, her seedy dress gone round the circle of fashion, so that it had almost come in again. Long and high waisted and rather severely flowing, it had once been black, but time had purpled it, and it was filthy. And yet, somehow, its absurd gentility survived. Every stitch had the shine of shabby aristocracy on it.

And even before that woman opened her mouth I knew precisely what her speech would be. I could have mimicked its thin-lipped nicety, its high-pitched cockney-cultured accent, the almost tragic effort with which it was so meticulously spoken.

Then we went in, and the house was a museum of crazy filth. Books and rolls of prints were piled and strewn over the floors and the peeling veneered card-tables. Apples lay in rotten parsimonious heaps on chairs and chests and floors and bureaux. The blinds were cock-eyed in the fly-marked windows. In the drawing-room an ancient piano of yellow wood and dumb keys stood askew in the middle of the room, strewn with gilt-edged prayer books and the foxed music-sheets of Edwardian songs. There was something unbelievably stupid and sinister about it. There was no purpose in it. That crazy jumble of genteel filth was like a shot from a shadowy and rather bad film.

Then suddenly I realised that it was mad: that only someone of

lunatic mentality could have piled up and lived with that extraordinary conglomeration of genteel rubbish. Even by itself it would have been crazy, but she believed in it. She saw it not simply as we saw it, as a mad jumble of decaying junk, but as it had been. "It's beautiful," she kept saying. "It's beautiful."

We bellowed, hands cupped to shout through her deafness. "We would like to look upstairs!—please!—if we may!—upstairs!"

"I beg your pardon?"

"Perhaps we might look upstairs!"

"The apples are so beautiful this year. The Lord Suffields are so beautiful."

"Please!" we shouted, "we would like to look upstairs! If we might intrude! Upstairs! At the bedrooms!"

"You see this Bible? It's Brown's Bible. Feel it. Look at the pictures. It's beautiful, isn't it beautiful? It's worth a lot of money. There's a picture of——"

"Yes, but could we go upstairs?"

"If you set up house you'll need a Bible. Would you like it? Would you buy it? It's beautiful."

Well, we would consider the Bible, but meanwhile—"Could we please go upstairs? Upstairs! The bedrooms! If you don't mind!"

"She's crackers," I said hopelessly.

I hoped she would not know the word, and she didn't, but she caught its implications. She opened the stairs door without any more trouble, and I said, quite quietly:

"That's a nice bureau."

"Yes," she said, with her squeaky, mad voice, "it's beautiful. Isn't it beautiful?"

It was the old word, but there was a change of attitude. She had heard me. Strange—her deafness to those repeated requests of ours to go upstairs. Perhaps she didn't want us to go upstairs? Perhaps there was some question of secrecy there?—feminine secrecy, something we ought not to see?—her bloomers hanging over an antique chair, some decayed pair of ancient stays lying on the counterpane, her nightdress?

I felt dubious. "Perhaps we ought not to go up?" I whispered.

"Oh! yes, come along," she said in a loud squeak. "You may come up."

So we went up into the upper darkness. Could she hear? Was she mad? Suddenly I looked at her. As she walked before us along the landing she took strides of extraordinary, almost masculine length. I looked at her hips. Was it the dress? They were curiously straight and narrow. Was it long years of virgin solitude, of no love and much squeezing of her body through the narrow spaces between chests and bureaux and pianos and tables? She looked extraordinarily like a man.

She took us into bedrooms, quickly, rather guiltily. She pushed open the door of one room with a curious fretfulness. Did we mind? She held the door open an inch or two. It was her room —we didn't mind? She did not want us to go in there. We caught a glimpse of crazy piles of ladies' magazines, old clothes, travelling trunks, books, papers, untidy bedclothes, jumbles of gloomy paintings in oils, all the crazy genteel muck all over again. Did we mind not going in? *It wasn't cleaned up.* The other rooms *were* clean, but not this one. "But it's a beautiful room," she said, "it's a beautiful room. You'll like it. It's so beautiful."

She took us, finally, into the uppermost darkness, to an attic lying under the very roof, and we saw there the dregs of her queer life, all the things she had lived on and had lived for, the things she had cherished and couldn't bring herself to throw away: many piles of empty sugar-boxes, of empty cartons of patent oatmeal, and again many gentlewomen's magazines, and then her travelling trunks, the clumsy jumbled relics of the days when she must have been a somebody, one of the Miss Somebodies, young and eligible, with chances and perhaps a look in her eye, and full hips, and some shape in her now ironed-out breasts. Those trunks had on them the strangest destinations: Natal, Cape Town, Gold Coast, Marseilles, Mentone, Singapore, Egypt, the Antipodes. Had she been so far? There was one, also, of strange length: flat, long, coffin-like. Painted black, it looked as though made to hold a body. Hurriedly, after looking at it, we went down.

And this woman, with her air of being one thing and trying to disguise herself as another, is the exaggerated ideal of earnest and spurious gentility. She is clinging hard to the idea of herself not as she was, but as she perhaps ought to have been and as she wished to be. But somewhere something has gone wrong. The ideal is clear enough, but the paraphernalia that supports it has got into a state of cranky disorder verging on mild lunacy. Trying to build up about herself the ramparts of superfine gentility, she has preserved and cherished every stitch and page and nail of things even faintly aristocratic, quite blind to the muck and jumble and craziness of it all, seeing only the ideal, worshipping only the silly godhead of a decaying but elegant world.

Such people, clinging hard to faded ideals, are surprisingly common still in country places, wherever industrialism has not penetrated. Their stage is small, and therefore all entrants on it must be carefully scrutinised. So, when you meet them, they put you through a sweet but rigid catechism. Do you know the Captain? they ask, as though there were only one captain. And when you reply No, you do not know the Captain, but you know a captain, it is not enough. It is different. It will not do. Then, since you come from X, you must know the Miss Scribbles? No, you do not know the Miss Scribbles and you begin to feel that your world, too, is incomplete. What do the Miss Scribbles do? And it seems that the Miss Scribbles do nothing and yet are, at the same time, not as other women. Then, since you are a writer, you must know Miss Cranford? And it turns out that Miss Cranford is herself a writer and has written fifty books and that neither you, nor anyone else, has ever heard of her. And so it goes on, a play running through an eternal number of acts, with its carefully cast players fencing and playing and whispering and sweet-smiling and back-biting through all the small dramas of parochial life. To you, an outsider, a stranger, it seems incomprehensible. Yet to the players, each guarding veritable rosaries of shining ideals, it means everything.

All villages are the same. Pretty, idyllic, sequestered, old-fashioned, pastoral, you may call them what you like, but they are all of them sweet-shelled nuts with small bitter kernels. The ideal of the pure and perfect village, what the guide books set out as an unsullied gem in God's own setting, is as much a myth as the ideal of alchemy. Generations of writers, either through fear or dishonesty or perhaps even want of knowledge, have painted the English village as a golden thing. And so it often is, as with the villages of the Ouse, in mere setting and form and architecture. In beauty of shape and scene, it has often no equal. But stone and thatch and tiles and trees make up the body simply. What of the spirit? And what, though we will not discuss it here, of the thatch which leaks, the sweet cottage with no drainage and a wooden privy, the water-logged floor, the bedrooms which have to be divided off by curtains so that boys can sleep on one side and girls the other or even parents on one side and children the other? The idyll begins to crack when you bear too hard on it. And it is not there at all, but goes through some paradoxical alchemic process of turning from gold to muck, if you should happen to be unfortunate enough to have to sit in that winter-blasted privy and sleep in that curtain-divided bedroom.

Angle is everything; and once you learn the trick of changing the angle, anything can be proved to be exactly the opposite of what it is. Thus for you, passing by, getting the angle of the sun right, the cast of elm-shadows perfect and so on, some cottage shines out in a perfection of beauty. But in it, chained to it, some poor devil cannot stand upright, can write his name with his fingers on the wall's wetness, can hear the rats running over his head at night, and must walk fifty yards, perhaps across the road, to his wretched privy. Your beauty has no meaning for him. He takes his picture from a different angle and the two results are cruelly different. Exposed, printed, described, set down in words, they would seem like descriptions of two different worlds.

So, for me, the villages of the Ouse remain completely delightful, serene little bunches of stone and thatch and coloured plaster on the river's edge, only because I have seen them, through many years, from one and the same angle. My exposures of them are all exteriors. I could, by guessing, by imagination, even by trickery, perhaps, make an interior exposure, but it would no longer be authentic. To get the angle right, I must live there, in the interior, and know not only what it looks like but what it feels like. For all sorts of reasons I cannot do it. So I stick to the exterior view: the broad river winding and winding, almost crazily, among its cattle-quiet pastures and primrose woods, the sleepy villages of cream and terracotta and white and strawberry-coloured plaster, the small churches among the trees, the masses of corn-thick reeds by the bridge-sides and the fishermen half asleep on their little floats in the drowsy afternoons.

Water Flowers and Water Creatures

I see the Ouse, always, in fact, under the high light of summer. I had my first sight of it, unexpectedly, across meadows, with the glimpse of a white mansion beyond its great reeds in the glaring August sun. It was the reeds which marked it out as something different and wonderful. Reeds in the Nene had for years been systematically cut down, and I had grown not to expect them on water. Suddenly, here was a stream crowded with reeds; they grew in great shining islands, in waving promontories, in bowed fringes along the brim, even in great dams sown like giant green corn across a whole breadth of water. I have never been able to get those reeds, so thick and gigantic, out of my mind. They gave the river some air of romantic aristocracy. They were so tall, except where wind and high water had elbowed and beaten them over, that they cut up the stream into sections, so that some part of it always lay hidden and in mystery. We walked along it for miles, and I remember being held in fascination, first by its width, then by the gloominess of the clay-blue shelf under the banks where it narrowed and deepened, and finally by something which had nothing really to do with the stream: the woods on its banks; the stream ran through woods and I found it hard to believe it. And it was here that I first became aware of the extraordinary sense of delicacy and yet of absolute permanence that water and trees can give to each other, of the water's apparent solidity against the cloudy willows that looked as if they were nothing but trees of smoke; then by the sturdiness of trees growing darkly together, in a gloomy summer regiment, against which the water was something ephemeral, of unterrestrial delicacy, hardly of earth. Trees have a way of, in a metaphorical sense, uplifting water. They transpose it to a higher plane. A single poplar, bending over, will make a transformation. Conversely, water dignifies trees, lights them up, rarefies their shapes, so that they are somehow suspended. Yet they stand, river and trees, in eternal contradiction of each other: the one transient and fluid and making a perpetual passage over some great length of earth, the other fixed and solid as a battlement and making no passage at all except the eternal passage from summer to summer, repeating the endless miracle of bud and leaf, greenness and death.

But if the trees on the Ouse astonished me, its flowers won me over completely. In places its water-lilies did, and still do, what the reeds do: they make great islands and promontories and fringes all about the stream, even blocking it with a vast dam of gold and white. I once knew a man who, in the blithe expectation of a serene holiday, chartered a rowing-boat and set out to navigate this piece of stream between the village of Harrold and the town of Bedford. He had given himself a week. Within two days, after scarcely any rowing at all but only an endless sweat of smashing a course through forests of reed and rush and water-lily and even of picking up his boat and carrying it, he gave it up. Nor was this his only obstacle. The distance between Harrold and Bedford, as the crow flies, would be, perhaps, ten miles. It looks nothing. Old ladies, no doubt, cycle it in an afternoon. But as the river flows, on the craziest of snaky courses, doubling in giant loops and ox-bows, it must be almost thirty miles. It is no wonder at all that the Ouse folk have never attempted its commercial navigation.

So it has an extra richness of flowers. By this I mean not only flowers that are purely water flowers, growing in the stream, but flowers that grow along the river-banks and about them, the flowers of two worlds, the border-line things. Loosestrife towers up all through late summer in magenta steeples just on the lip of water, that rather flamboyant colour softened down by the water itself, by the corn-colour of the burnt-up grass and, where it still persists, by the cream fluffed feathers of meadowsweet. Wild iris are over by then. The green seeds are fattening to pod, and rushes are rising in dark sienna platoons, stiff and artificial, military in their sword-straightness and uniformity. They were held, once, in vast esteem for the mantelpiece, in winter; and I remember we coveted them and I thought they were like the war drumsticks of a savage people. About the same time, July and August, water-mint edges every river and brook and ditch with a cloud-embroidery of mauve. It smells too fiercely for me, a contradictory little plant, so mild in flower, so astringent and harsh in scent. Willow herb is there like some wild sowing of pink-flowered corn. They call it Codlins and Cream, I can't see why, and it has been almost ousted now by its finer namesake, the rose-bay willow herb, a plant that has swept England like a pink fire. Frothing seed, it pinks whole acres in wild places. The old willow herb is never so prodigal; it clings to water. It is a lovely thing but, like almost all late summer flowers, unlovable. It is the earlier blossomings, both of tree and flower, that go to the heart: the great water-fed tussocks of the primroses full-blown on the water-edge, the bell-headed cowslips, golden, deep wine-scented, the butter-varnished bowls of king-cups, the small vaporous flowers of the mauve lady-smocks. They have the pristine delicacy of first morning in them, a purity and clarity never matched by all the heavy spangling and wealth of later summer. Cool suns give them cool colours and scents, some vitalising freshness of look and perfume quite removed from the high summer creams and yellows and purples, with their too dreamy, almost narcotic odours.

But all these are not water flowers truly; they are happy on land and in marshy places. They are the water's embroideries. They run through all the colours, from the enamel blue of water forget-me-not through the golds and creams of kingcup and cowslip and meadowsweet to the pinks and purples of willow herb and loose-strife. But those water flowers, that can grow only in water, have no colour like this. It is as though water had some exceedingly refining influence, some power of miraculous cleansing, leaving only white, with certain pink species and yellow water-lily and yellow mimulus as inglorious and glorious exceptions. Even yellow water-lilies are not spectacular. This leaves only that little lizard-bellied yellow monkey-musk, with its soft blood-spotted trumpets, and even that is happy sometimes on land as well as water. There are few other water flowers, in England, that break the rule of white. In fact, it would seem odd and in some way out of harmony with English waters to come suddenly upon some scarlet reach of water-poppy, a blue bay of water-cornflowers, some orange island of water-marigold. It seems right, somchow, for English water flowers to have a water delicacy, a northern and almost icy purity of colourlessness.

So we get many fragile islands of quiet-flowering water-weed, of which water-ranunculus is the best and strangest. Floating densely, white-flowered, almost like a white buttercup, it has this curious quality: that its leaves change their shape above water. Below water they are like the leaves of crow's-foot; they branch out, airy, many-fingered, almost like sea-weed. Above it, they become solid, without any airiness and with the shape of clover. Sometimes, when a leaf is cut across by the water-line, it will take on both shapes, the under-water fingers below, the clover-shape above. In its full best, in early summer, this flower effaces water, transforms it into one solid mass of shining white and green, like some mossy island of white saxifrage.

But it is like some delicate dress rehearsal, a mere show of puppet flowers, as compared with the full show of midsummer. In June and July it is as though the small flowers of the water-ranunculus are turned, by some magic, into great flowers of china: the water-lilies crowd all over the stream and dominate it. They are absolute aristocrats, not only among water flowers simply, but among all English wild flowers at all. On the Ouse, on the reaches below Stevington, they dam the stream with great stretches, like floating magnolias, swan-white. They conjure a multitude of similes; they are so simple and perfect, both in colouring and shape, that they defeat and tangle metaphor. Closed, not yet free of water, they come up exactly like creamy-green buds of magnolia, unwrithing themselves from stems that are like a tangle of water-snakes. Half open, more yellow than white, more stamen than petal, they are like white China peonies. And then, full open, in full sun, they shine from a distance like nothing so much as a vast frying of eggs turned out in the great olive platters of the leaf-pods. It is a simile of shocking banality, but it springs spontaneously to mind, and the spontaneity of similes is everything. And then, closer, they are like great cups of milk-white glass, the bright concentration of stamens almost luminous, in the sun, with pollen-fire. They look very unreal then, unreal and unattainable, not flowers so much as modellings of flowers. They have a kind of touch-me-not artificiality about them, an unearthly and visionary fragility.

They are flowers which will go on for many weeks. Yet we would always sit and look at them, with steadfast delight, for hours on end, as though they were somehow ephemeral, too good to be true, not to be trusted to remain. We would sit captivated by

the double fascination of the river, with the summer light on it, and the countless flowers. And we would get, often, some piece of treble fascination: not only of flowers and water, but of birds and flowers and water, with a kingfisher leaping across the stream and lilies, in a flight of blue electricity, or with a pair of swans waltzing with slow-motion regality downstream, birds and flowers finding their own matchless white for once matched in each other. We once saw, also, a pike lying like a still torpedo beyond the fringe of lilies, a biggish fellow, sunning himself in the hot afternoon just under the surface of water. It is customary to think of fish as creatures of perpetual restlessness, never still; but there is no stillness like the stillness of a sunning pike. He lies as stiff and immobile as a rod of yellowish steel. No bird, and I believe no animal, attains that same perfection of rigidity. It is at once dynamic and sinister. It contains a terrific potentiality of speed and strength. Yet it looks, at first sight, a sleepy and gentle pose, almost feline, the mere silky shadow of a great leaf drowning dimly in the sun-clear water.

I once saw there, also, two other pieces of treble delight: first, an endless procession, just over the area of lilies, of small sapphire dragonflies, a continuous play of blue gauze over the snowy flowers above the sun-glassy water. It was all confined, in true dragonfly fashion, to one small space. It was a continuous turning and returning, an endless darting, poising, striking and hovering, so swift that it was often lost in sunlight. It was like a crazy flight of almost invisible humming-birds. It never rested. And poised in that miraculous act of hovering, wings invisible, bodies like tiny fingers of blue steel, these small fragile creatures had exactly the same suspended power, the same dynamic and thrilling immobility, as the pike lying in wait in the water.

The other sight was also blue, and I had it on land, on the grass. Walking, I saw ahead of me a space of forget-me-nots. As I approached they grew not more clear, as they should have done, but curiously vaporous. Then I saw that they were not tall enough for forget-me-nots; they clung to earth like speedwell. And then, when I was five yards away, all of a sudden they took wing. They rose up in a small blue cloud of powder: a large host of turquoise butterflies, a miraculous crowd of pale-blue flying ghosts. They were merely Common Blues, but that sudden spontaneity of flight, and its delicious blue airiness, was ethereal.

Which brings up, naturally, things in crowds. There is some strange beauty, combined often with stupidity or recklessness or even madness, in the behaviour of wild creatures gathered together. A single hare—and he often seems to me to be almost the most attractive of English wild animals, since there is nothing so good and glorious as the leap of a hare's wild-eyed bolting—will behave with great sanity of purpose, straightforwardly, tearing to escape across corn or grass or ploughed land on a course as fixed and straight as a bullet's. Running from danger, indeed, he often

runs straight into danger because of the fixedness of his flight. He is caught for this reason. He is the victim of a too direct purpose. But in spring, gathered together, hares behave with an inexplicable lunacy that is like some idiotic mumming play. I have often seen, about the Nene, a crowd of six or ten in a field of rough grass, in March, behaving with a super-madness that was both baffling and comic. They would tear round and round in the field in spasmodic broken circles as though being chased by the ghosts of diabolical whippets: no purpose in it, no end, no beginning, only a mad careering to each other and away from each other and to nowhere at all. It was a great silly gambolling and leaping, as though the field were an asylum for moon-struck hares. Rabbits will behave similarly, though not so madly. They are mere feeble imitators, but even they, in spring crowds, will leap like lambs.

Similarly with most birds and butterflies and animals that flock together. They have special and individual moments of strange crowd behaviour: the great evening flight and settling and abrupt uprising, almost like an explosion, of starlings; the pretty twittering silliness of linnets; the solemn winter love-play of blackbirds, six or even ten in a gang, feeding on grass, eyeing each other, making discreet rushes and advances, almost nonconformist in their black suspicion and seriousness; the comic cackling of rooks in times of storm; the occasional savagery of stoats hunting by pack.

But water creatures, fish especially, seem different. Except the water boatmen, rowing as in a comic strip across the water surface, in a delicious piece of comic seriousness, the crowds of water creatures behave with more design, as though drilled, as though perhaps under the domination of water. Even minnows will lie in small poised companies, in level order, all flicking off in one direction at the approach of danger. Schools of trout lie in sunlight as still as painted leaves, motionless against the current, keeping the same place for hours on end by the exercise of an astonishing strength, flashing off like clockwork darts at the fall of a shadow. It is as though intense training were essential for the perfection of the machinery of escape. Watching a school of trout, indeed, seeing it move off at an electric diagonal, to vanish in a flash, you begin to marvel that man, using his primitive and clumsy devices, should ever catch any fish at all.

Against the lovely collective motions of fish, snakes in water look uncommonly sluggish. They seem to lose their sinuousness and go along in a slow silver worming, as if not quite in their element. In bright water, silvered by sun, they move invisibly except for the oval crafty head swinging along like a piece of chequered steel. They delight in the camouflage of lilies, lying among the polished green stems with casual motionlessness, quite indistinguishable. Then they give themselves away by the habit of lying with their heads on the leafpads, drowsing, softly curled, so light that the leaf is still dry except for its habitual blobs of quicksilver. They move with extreme quietness, with much less noise than on land. But for all their silvery loveliness they look somehow dangerously charged, silkily sinister. And sometimes, with bodies invisible, their approach is quite startling. It seems as if the head, disembodied, is swimming alone, moving with perfect instinct, like a torn leg of a fly after the body has been destroyed.

Flowers of Childhood

By the beginning of June the grasses are higher than the knees of children; the bull-daisies begin to flower at their waists. The bull-daisy, the moon-daisy of many districts, the dog-daisy of others and the wild marguerite of flower books, is almost the largest of children's flowers, the white moon among the many little honeyed constellations of their dearest treasures. It stands at the zenith of the child's flower year, the full flower moon in a sky crowded with a million buttercup stars and countless milky ways of white nettle and kex and rose and clover. The child seems to have no use for larger or taller flowers. The flowers of trees are beyond its reach, just as the flowers of garden are forbidden it. It has only this miniature kind of earth, this summer firmament of grass filled with its many-coloured stars.

It is hard to say where in the year the flowers of childhood begin. With March and the yellow coltsfoot perhaps; more likely with April and the violet. The first search is for the violet, for the white buds hanging in the cold grass along the still bare hedge-sides, the purest of flowers, like little aristocratic magnolias of snowdrop shape, more precious even than the dark violets that cover the wood-earth between the primroses and the budding bluebells and the green flowered dog's mercury like a settling of purple butter-flies. The violet is the enigmatic little aristocrat among spring flowers; there is something secretive and essentially passionate about it. It is almost foreign to spring; it seems to belong in essence to the scent and heat of July. And there is something in that secrecy and escape that the child loves. To escape and find the violet secretly is a joy which is never recaptured even with the cowslip

and the rose, and which remains with it and renews itself long after it is a child no longer.

So with the anemone and the bluebell and the primrose. They are not only children's flowers; they are universal. The child has no other names for them than the names of long tradition. It is only with the flowers of insignificance, the weeds, that the child comes into a world perfectly its own, loaded with a sweetness of darling names coined by long affection and imagination: titty-bottles and totty-grass, scent-bottles and grannies' night-caps, kiss-me-quick and pull-your-grannie's-eyes-out. They are flowers which it may never know by another name. And since many of them are perfect names there seems no reason why it ever should. For white campion, beautiful in itself, can never express the shape and colour and even the time of its flowering as grannies' night-cap does. And I have never troubled to find out for myself the classic names of totty-grass, that little hair-stemmed grass with reddish quivering beads of flower which comes in May and June, or of scent-bottles, which break into lilac cocoons of powdery flower in the deep grass of summer, simply because the names I gave to them in childhood have long since seemed to me perfect names. And for the same reason speedwell is still pull-your-grannie's-eyes-out and the name still the reason why I never gather it. And the titty-bottles of the red clover are still sweet to suck.

And the flowers which may be sucked are many. There are infinitesimal drops of winy nectar in the bell-hearts of cowslip and primrose; the clover flowers are little pinkish breasts that give honey-suck; the flowers of the white nettle are cool creamy horns holding a single drop of sweetness. The child knows the honey-hearted flowers by instinct; the bluebell is never sucked, nor the foxglove, nor the buttercup. It is something unconscious; the child knows the sweet from the unsweet as clearly in its heart as it knows sun from shadow. The kingcup is pure gold, the kex is living lace, the daisy makes a chain of pink and silver, but they lack that secret sweetness which for the child is far lovelier than rarity or colour or even scent.

And when finally that sweetness and colour and scent fuse into the summery passion of hay-time, the loveliness of the child's flower year, like our own, reaches its height. The meadow grass is a forest rich with blossoms whose names the botanist could never have coined in a month of studious Sundays: the ragged robins like torn pink petticoats in marshy places, the golden egg-and-bacon of the kidney vetch, the pink and white sunshades of convolvulus, the go-to-bed-at-noons, and with them all the unaccountable glory of moon-daisy and clover and meadowsweet and orchis whose sweetness is only outdone by the sweetness of the mown grass itself. The child for a little while is in its heaven; its sky is covered with stars as thick as grass and with a million moons that shine most gloriously in sunlight. The wild rose is out, the honeysuckle buds are half-hidden by the thickness of full leaves, the poppies are dawning crimson in the young corn. The flowering places of wood-sides and hedge-sides are hiding-places—to hide in still silence in the deep flowering grass is something altogether un-equalled in suspense and delight. The child's flower world expands almost beyond it. There are flowers it cannot touch. The willow herb rises in steeples of pink, the loosestrife in trees of purple. And the little aristocratic violets of April lie forgotten in the memory like cold jewels of purple and white.

But suddenly the mower changes it all. The meadows by the

rivers are no longer luscious; the grass is burnt up in the heat of July. The ditches and hedge-sides alone remain untouched, creamy aisles of meadowsweet and parsley and seeding grass. There are flowers, many flowers in fact, yellower and more brilliant than the sunlight itself, but a little of the midsummer wonder has gone.

It is not until harvest that that wonder renews itself and the child comes fully into its own again. For the binder, unlike the mower, leaves behind it a little spring-time of flowers, all the humble miniatures that the knife cannot touch and which the child loves: scarlet pimpernel and speedwell and wild camomile and centaury and sunshade and pansy, a kind of second April in the heat of harvest-time, a paradox of blossoming in the scorched barrenness of the stubbles.

And that miniature flowering, except for chance blossoms of daisy and honeysuckle and buttercup, virtually ends the child's flower year. The wonder and lusciousness of April and June are gone and can never be recaptured—even if it ever occurred to a child to try to recapture them. It is perhaps only for us that the desire for recapture becomes a reality. We get into the habit of longing for springs that have gone. We look into the faces of children and violets and half see ourselves as we were in the summers of another world.

The Water-Mill

Water shares with woods some power of tranquillising the spirit, of quietening it almost to a point of dissolving it away; so that nearly all the best enjoyment of a piece of water comes from the mere act of sitting near it and doing nothing at all. It must surely be this power which attracts human beings in thousands to narrow strips of sand and shingle all over the world, which lures them to sit there, hot and crowded, and gaze for hours at the expanses of sea and sky. The eating of whelks and winkles, the drinking of beer, the wearing of cock-eyed hats, the promenading, the riding of donkeys, even the parade of nudity could all be done elsewhere. There is no law, so far as I know, to prevent men riding donkeys, while wearing the hats of American sailors, up and down the country lanes of England. There is nothing to stop a collective eating of whelks and winkles on commons and roadsides. And even keepers might look without hostility perhaps, on ladies birds'-nesting in bathing costumes. But these things are not done, and the men and women who did do them would probably be locked up for lunacy. But by water such expressions of light-heartedness are natural. Especially the business of merely sitting still and doing nothing at all is natural. "Sit still," a man will say, "what are we here for?" Yet this man would no more dream of sitting still in the middle of a grass field and doing nothing but gaze at the sky than he would of playing football with his Sunday hat. And if you asked a hundred people sitting in a seashore attitude of tranquil negation what they were up to, what would they reply? "We're sunbathing, we're resting, we're taking it easy." They might even reply that they were doing nothing at all.

All this is true, in a lesser way, of rivers. And this tranquillising effect, almost a kind of mild hypnotism, becomes deeper and stronger as a river gets wider and wider. The broader a river gets the more soothing it gets. Space is restful; and a great space of one kind of thing, of grass or sky, corn or landscape, or water especially, can be profoundly restful. When a river is small the eye is distracted, caught up by the surrounding colour and motion of tree and grass and flower and bird. When it is very small, only a brook, a stream is beautiful and arresting not simply for itself, as a flowing course of water, but because of the closeness of the beauty of other things, of reed and sedge, of purple-budded alders, of crabs in blossom, of the cream waterfalls of may, of flags and cresses, things without which it would remain a mere ditch, a gulley. There is so little water and so much land that the effect of the water is almost shallow itself. It produces quick, light, merry emotions, without any of that effect of deep pleasure and power or magnetism or mystery or profound tranquillity aroused by a great breadth of water.

But there comes also a point, in going down the river, where fascination deepens to stupefaction, where there is too much altogether of tranquillity, where the proportion of water to land goes beyond the point of perfection. For this reason I feel sure of two things: that the best rivers, like the best woods, are not large; and that the best of any river, large or small, lies in its middle course, somewhere midway between source and sea. Thus I prefer Ouse to Forth; Thames and Seine and Neckar to Rhine; just as I think I might very well prefer Rhine to Volga if I were to see the Volga, or Volga to Mississippi.

A river in its middle reaches seems to have the best of two worlds. It is no longer playful and insignificant. It is large but not too large, important but not too important. It is arresting and tranquillising at the same time. It can still be bridged with ease, and small bridges, like small rivers, are so often better than large. Small country mills line its banks, and what is true of bridges is still truer of mills. It has altogether an intimacy about its life that later, nearer the sea, it seems to lose. As it nears the sea its greater breadth demands that it should be used, and bang go its flowers, its great islands and peninsulas of rushes, its silted dams of stone and branches making small weirs and waterfalls, its drunken willows and poplars stooping dangerously and beautifully across it. The small wharves, small pubs and the small villages of colour-washed plaster and stone begin to be replaced by warehouses and factories. The mills begin to look like great forlorn chalk-dusty tenements. Railways begin to run down to the waterside. There is a spewing of smoke, discharging and loading of coal, the clack and smack of planked-down timber. Small ships, red-sailed, begin to appear and the little pleasure boats, plush-cushioned, fancy-named, begin to look ridiculous. There is a new element: the sea. It begins to colour, ever so faintly, the faces of ships, the dust of wharves, the names of pubs. There is a clash and mingling of elements. Pleasure is hit by commerce. Green meadows are swamped by docks and jetties. Masts and sails replace the willows. Water-lilies, the purple-bloomed catkins of alder, the skeins of green girls'-hair reed, become memories. At the marriage of river and sea springs a new life, bastard, lusty, crude, in its own way romantic—the river-port. It replaces the river-town, the place which takes a snobbish pride in its river, lining its banks with public gardens, with strips of geraniums blazing on white promenades, and seats on which you may sit to watch the passage of sweating boating parties, white-vested eights, drifting lovers. The port has no relation to all this. It is uncouth, mucky, swaggering: a place, so to speak, that wipes its mouth on the back of its hand and spits, without nicety of feeling, in the gutter. A place, in fact, not only of new colour and appearance, but of new manners. It has no time for the holding of regattas, the playing of bands in floating bandstands, for fairy lights and all the pretty paraphernalia of up-river places. It has new and unbeautiful virility, all the fascination of a slightly shady romance.

All this is good, but in the evolution of it so much has gone. The wild life has vanished, and with it the special feeling of solitude, of width and tranquillity, that goes with the middle distances of the stream. Summer comes to the port and there is, except in the sweat of bodies and the white fierceness of pavements, no difference. There is no smell of mown grass, of meadows drowsy with June heat. Winter freezes and is a nuisance: there is no exhilaration of red-sunned afternoons on ice, no beauty of sugared sedges and trees. The river rises and floods and is a scare, a danger; there is no magnificent forlorn wildness of sky-grey

flood waters. There remain no animals except rats, no birds but seagulls.

One of the best of all the features of the middle river has gone too: the country mill. Nothing stands in its place. The great dust-whitened prisons of port quay-sides have as much relation to it as blast furnaces to the shops of blacksmiths. The country mill is an individual thing, a landmark. It occupies, on the river, something of the position of inns and churches on the road, and it makes, with them, that staunch triangle of religion and malt and corn on which so much of the history of these islands has been built up. Mills and millers, inns and innkeepers, parsons and pulpits have been recurring features in the solid architecture of English life since before Chaucer gave us that gorgeous and supreme story of a mill and its miller.

Reading that story, I see it, always, enacted behind the stone walls of the mill to which we, twenty-five years ago, took the year's harvest to be ground. It was my privilege, then, to take some part in every act which went towards making the bread I ate. I helped set the brushes of the corn-drill; I led the horse for the drilling; I watched for the young corn to shoot; I helped hoe and roll it; I helped sheaf and bond it, fashioning the bonds according to the ancient and simple local pattern; I helped shock and carry it, staggering about with the great bearded shocks twice as large as myself, cutting my shins on the stubbles, leading the horse; I helped stack and thresh it; I let the bright gold grain run through my fingers as we sacked it. And then, in time, I sat on the fat piled sacks when we drove the cart down the valley, to the mill on the Nene, for the year's milling. Later still, I ran for the yeast, which was to leaven that rich dark flour, and I can smell on my hands, still, the queer beery smell of barm, and I can see on the barm itself the criss-crossing print of its coarse muslin, and I can taste, above all, the bread itself, sweet, dark, almost the colour of rye bread, very nearly the colour of the earth which had grown it.

And I see, with the same clarity and much of the same pleasure, the mill itself. It stands, now, in dismal ruin; but it stood, then, in prosperous security, fairly large, of stone, with a wide ring of doddle-willows standing like dumpy besoms all about the mill-pool. The whole place had some air of benign solidity and timeless security, but not quietness. All day and all night there was the ceaseless smashing down of water through the mill-races. The water tore and spewed out from under the arches in black polished arcs that were churned suddenly to a great creamy boil of froth, which spread out all across the mill-pool in a simmering and bubbling of swirling currents and eddies. This was in normal weather. But after rain, in times of flood, there was no mill-pool. It was one with floods. And there were almost no arches. They were drowned under great torrents, except perhaps for a narrow aperture at the very crest of the circle. Water boiled and spewed everywhere, flooding everything: mill-yard and garden and road and, I feel sure, mill itself. For, years afterwards, when decay had set in, I went over the mill, and everywhere I could smell that queer fungoid smell, watery and rotten, that comes only after centuries of permeation by water, the smell of damp-rotted boards, damp-mouldered wallpaper, damp-frowsy linen closets, damp-soaked bricks. The deserted rooms were funereal. The great kitchen floor slabs, smooth as horn, were like tomb-stones. The smell and feel of water had grown into a power. Beside it the corruption of moth and rust was gentle. Moth and rust are local, but this strange power of water was wholesale, had permeated everything, was increasing. And when you looked out of the window of the place, and round it, you saw the reason why. The mill was virtually built on water. It was an island connected by a peninsula of a cart-track with the road outside. The mill-races ran underneath it, and the mill-wheel churned and splashed against its wall in great slow revolutions of silver and slime. The backwater ran past its very windows. Millions of tons of water, and then millions, must have sluiced past it and under it. In winter, perched up on its grassy island, surrounded by its witch-broom willows half-drowned in water, it had all the desolate air of housing some forlorn and mouldy legend.

It was about this time, when I made my first and only tour of its interior, that they began to try and pull it down. It was, it seemed, unsafe. Exactly how absurd this was I shall show in a moment. And since milling was no longer much done in the antique way, as by Chaucer's miller, no one wanted the mill for work, still less for habitation. So it was sold, and men came and looked at it, and subsequently carts came down, and labourers, and there was a smashing of pickaxes. The roof came off, and there was a stark exposure of wallpaper, with faded roses trailing to the sky. And then it appeared, as it so often appears, that the man who put up the house had far more sense than those who were pulling it down. Looking ahead, seeing upon him, perhaps, two or three hundred years of work and winter floods and tempest, he had built his walls of immense thickness. They stood as solid as the walls of prisons. These were the walls that had seemed unsafe. Then, as the pickaxes laboured, labour costs went up, and the job became a bad egg. The contractor got frightened or tired, and finally it was left to stand, more forlorn than ever, roofless, rosy wallpaper wind-torn and rain-splashed, windows like skeletons. It was still, apparently, unsafe, and there it still stands, an absolute mockery of itself, useless, ruined, looking at flood-time less like a mill than some broken bit of monastic remains on the shore of a lake.

But the really impressive features of that mill were not the walls, but the mill-stones and the mill-wheel. Those vast upper and nether stones, like great stone moons, would be a night-mare to a man who made his living by building those present-day houses in which, as their tenants say, the walls are so thick that a man can hear the snoring of his neighbour. What has a builder like that to do with those primitive bits of stone machinery? I saw them lying on the upper floor of the mill, worn to the smoothness of iron by time and work, and they reminded me of Biblical illustrations. They had scarcely, since the time of Joseph, been superseded. They were like the great wheels of chariots. And outside, the wheel that drove them looked Biblical too. Water and stone, making power, was one of man's first and most timeless bits of ingenuity, and the rubbing of stone and corn must be one of the few sounds of man-devised things that has come down, unchanged, through many thousand years. The work of small-town contractors,

putting up red-brick shacks and pocketing the pence, begins to look very silly beside such things. There can hardly be another human device, still in use, that has such primitive origins as this rubbing of one stone against another. Water driving stone, stone grinding flour, flour making bread—these are the links between civilisations.

And the making of water-wheels still continues. This, in a highly mechanised age, seems rather surprising. A man does not need a new water-wheel, if he needs one at all, every week. Water-wheels, like church bells, last for what is, as far as we need trouble about it, eternity.

So I was glad to see a man, last summer, making a water-wheel. He was a man who also, as it happened, made church bells. Apart from the similarity, the closeness, of church and mill, perhaps there is also some similarity between bell and wheel? Both are round; both are instruments of music; both are mere useless bits of ornament without the contact of outside power. But it seems to go no further. There is no similarity between the music of bells and the music of water-wheels except, perhaps, their melancholy. And beside the massive architecture of a water-wheel, a bell, however big, is a mere piece of prettiness. If all the bells in Christendom had long since been melted down we should hardly be worse off. But the water-wheel has been for countless centuries a piece of essential machinery without which sowing and ploughing and reaping and harvesting would have been as useless as flour itself without an oven. Bells, like the prayers to which they call us, are a matter of taste. Water-wheels, combined with their twin stones, are part of the mechanism of necessity, cogs in man's machine for keeping himself alive.

This wheel-maker, when I saw him, had his wheel in sections, ready to assemble. It was September and the sections were spread out on a lawn, under an apple tree. The wheel was to be twenty-seven feet in diameter and was to replace some ancient affair of wood, at last worn out. In time its iron would be turned by water to the colour of wood, to that same green slime-skinned colour which covers locks and bridges and stones and boat bottoms. It was to be used, I think, for the generation of electric power, but the principle was the same, the same primitive revolution of wheel by water as ever.

There must be hundreds of dead and dumb mill-wheels, time-mossy, up and down this country. The windmill, a less ancient device in England at any rate, still flourishes, but the water-wheel has come, virtually, to what looks like a permanent standstill. Mills have been turned to farm-houses, and corn, by a queer irony, is grown within sight of the mill-race only to be taken elsewhere for its grinding. It is a curious paradox. But who wants to be chained to the melancholy thunder of a water-wheel? to that continuous thunder, thunder, swisha, thunder, thunder, shisha, thunder, all day long. No wonder, perhaps, that millers slid a hand into the sack which was not theirs? It was hard, perhaps, to resist the chance of compensation for being chained to that curiously melancholy sound, and, worse still, to the corruption of too much water, with the silent eating away of bones, the damping of spirits, the slow saturation of stone and wood and the final stretching on the rack of rheumatics. And why, anyway, should the miller have been singled out, in that delicate matter of business sleight-of-hand, from other men?

The Lace-Makers

The Ouse and the Nene, dissimilar in so many things, are bound together, curiously enough, by an art which flourishes scarcely anywhere else in England. Since it is an art which was, in origins, and still is, in essence, foreign to England, it is all the more remarkable that these two valleys, one rural and one industrial, should have fostered it with equal distinction. All along the Ouse, from Buckinghamshire down through Bedfordshire and on into Huntingdonshire, and all down the Nene, on a parallel line, little old women, looking appropriately as if they had come out of Dutch paintings, are still faithfully devoted to this lovely art, the art of making lace on pillows. These women are almost all old and they are the last of their kind. They have a look of seeming to be immemorial, with their lace caps, white hair, Rembrandt faces and skinny yellow hands, whereas they are, in reality, not only dying themselves but devoted to a dying art. Their immemoriality is a myth. They will not endure, and unless something in the way of a small revolution happens, their art will flutter out like a candle with them. This loss to English rural arts will be much the same as

117

if the writing of lyric poetry had died with Herrick. For of all English country arts this lace-making is indisputably the most delicate and fascinating. There is a quality of mystery about it, and the lace itself is a miracle of beauty. There is no other art quite so simple-looking and artless and yet so intricate and miraculous, so apparently aimless and yet so faithful to a thousand rigid principles.

Lace-making holds its distinction of place for several reasons. First, it is not only an art but a history, and not only a history but also a romance and a tragedy. Secondly, it is surprisingly delicate and difficult, learned only by great patience and trial and perseverance and ingenuity. Thirdly, its products are superb; pillow lace stands in relation to the rest of rural crafts exactly where poetry stands in relation to the rest of literature; at its best it is pure lyricism. Finally, apart from other things, it is the only craft I know of which the tools themselves are also works of art and histories and, at their best, bits of lyricism too.

On top of all these eulogies, none of which are extravagant, it is ironical to have to confess that the art is not really English at all. It has been English for four hundred years, but its origins are Flemish and French. It would be remarkable, in fact, if such a delicate art were English in origin. It is altogether too dainty and fanciful; its intricacies are carried to rather too rare a point of art. What is greatly to the credit of the English nature, as personified by the people of the Nene and the Ouse, is the genius with which it adapted, nourished and even improved an art which was essentially foreign to it.

It's an ill wind, even a dictatorship, that blows no good, and it was virtually a dictatorship, in 1567, and another, in 1572, that brought lace-making to this country. In 1556 Philip II of Spain succeeded Charles V of Spain as ruler of the Low Countries, and a peaceful country became a bloody country. Philip, like all dictators, ancient or modern, royal or common, believed in the shedding of a little blood. And in 1567 there ensued what is now, with almost medical propriety, called a purge but what was then, more plainly, called a massacre. Those who escaped that occasion, about 100,000 in all and, of course, Protestants, came to England, and they brought lace-making with them.

They drifted, for some not very clear reason, to Bedfordshire. In 1572, when that other and more famous purge occurred, the massacre of the Huguenots in France, the surviving lace-makers, mostly from Mechlin and Lille, drifted almost in the same direction, to Northamptonshire and Buckinghamshire. And those three counties are, still, except for a corner of Devonshire, the exclusive home of English pillow-lace.

Thus the history of lace-making is, from the first, drenched in blood. Later, much later, it was to be drenched in tears, not idle tears or even very catastrophic tears, but the miserable tears of small children working very early and very late in dark Victorian lace-schools at pillows they were not big enough to lift. Later, too, I have no doubt that other tears fell, the tears of old women forced to sell the most beautiful lace in the world to hucksters who squeezed them down to a last damnable farthing. One single bead of intricate Buckinghamshire point-ground lace takes hours of concentrated and expert work, yet I have seen such lace, three inches wide, for which the best huckster's price was eighteenpence a yard. No wonder its creator declared bitterly: "I'll go into the damn fields and spud turnips afore I make another blessed stitch at that price."

That same little woman, eighty-five years old and still giving lace lessons, suffers, though she does not know it, from claustrophobia, the fear of confined spaces. "When I was a mite of five I went to lace-school. One day I was too unwell to do my pattern. I said I couldn't do it. The teacher said: 'You'll do it or you shall be locked in the barn.' And now if you were to lock me in a room I should go mad! I've suffered for it all my life."

Yet without that early training and bitter concentration her art would never have been so fine. Lace-making is not learned in five minutes, and it is best learnt by the very young. Jesuits and lace-teachers had one thing in common: they took their pupils early and what they taught was never forgotten. If they taught by cruelty one can only point, in consolation and even vindication, to the results. The process of making lace on a pillow is difficult to describe, let alone to learn. It is one of those arts that look charming and simple, but which is, in reality, intricately difficult.

First, anyway, there is the pillow. Sausage shaped, looking rather like a soldier's kit-bag, it is stuffed with straw—with, if you please, a truss of straw, a truss being half a hundredweight. That straw is hammered and beaten down with a hammer until the pillow is like a pillow of iron.

The pillow stands on a wooden rest, a sort of trestle, waist high. Then, over the curve of the pillow, goes the parchment. On the parchment is the pattern, pricked out with pins and sometimes also with ink.

After that the processes are, to the lay mind, nothing but mysterious. You may watch a lace-maker until your eyes drop out, but if you do not know you do not know, and there it is. You will see the bone and wooden bobbins and their cottons flick and rattle in and out of place, and you will see the flash of pins moved and marshalled in order to make the stitches, but that, roughly, is as much as you ever will see. The bobbins move so rapidly that their manipulations seem like the jingling and rattling of someone gone quite crazy.

Those bobbins, next to the lace itself, are the supreme attraction of the art. They are, as I say, the only tools of any art that I know which are themselves works of art.

They fall, roughly, into two types: the bone and the wooden. An average bobbin is simply a piece of bone or wood, crudely or intricately carved, about three or four inches long. It looks like a miniature stair balustrade. On the bottom end of it is wired a ringlet of beads, a spangle. It will contain from one to nine beads:

turquoise and rose and milk and plum and amber, some as big as and very like robins' eggs, some no bigger than peas. All are delightful. There are, occasionally, special spangles. There is a bird-cage spangle: a single large bead contained in a cage of tiny beads of rainbow colours. There was, once, a famous spangle of a single enormous bead called Kitty Fisher's Eye, named after the actress.

But it is the bobbins themselves that are really pieces of history. In the old days bobbins were either carved at home or bought from a travelling dealer. If they were home-made they were almost always wooden, delicately carved out of rosewood, maple, plum, apple, laburnum, yew, apricot, box, cherry, blackthorn, even ebony.

If they were bought they were, mostly, of bone. Now a bone bobbin, being white, will take a design in colours. Therefore it became the fashion not only to decorate bone bobbins but to inscribe them. When dealers came round to take orders for new bobbins they took orders for inscriptions too. A baby had been born—inscribe its name on the bobbin. Someone had been married—mark the occasion and the date on the bobbin. Someone had died—let him have a bobbin memorial.

And gradually this game of inscribing and decorating bobbins grew to almost crazy proportions. Lace-makers began to inscribe on their bobbins not only births and deaths and marriages and betrothals, but sweet nonsense and prayers, hopes and fears, verses and texts, puzzles and songs, and, finally, murders and suicides.

When I first saw a murder bobbin I was shocked and embarrassed. It commemorated, I felt, some awful event in the family. Now I know better.

I cleared up the mystery by talking to two old Northampton-shire ladies, one nearly ninety and as hearty as a chicken, the other younger but deaf.

"Oh! whenever there was a murder and the murderer was hung in Bedford Gaol we had his name put on a bobbin, that's all. Ain't that right, Miss Perkins?"

"Eh?"

"I say we had all the murderers put on bobbins, didn't we? You came with me to see old Joseph Castle hung, didn't you?"

"Eh?"

"I say you came to see old Joseph Castle hung at Bedford, didn't you? You remember—up he went and then all of a pop he was gone. It was fourpence to have a murderer put on a bobbin," she said to me.

The airy callousness of these old ladies was something to think about. Later, I was able to buy a Joseph Castle bobbin—"Joseph Castle, Hung 1860"—and to discover, too, that Castle came from Luton and murdered his wife. On the March night when he was hanged the relatives of the murdered woman held a party. Every-one who went to that party had a bobbin inscribed with Castle's name.

The variation of bobbin designs and inscriptions is immense. Inscriptions are done in scarlet, scarlet and black, black; vertically, horizontally, spiral-fashion. They record all manner of family and local histories, of personal hopes and loves and fears and tragedies and aspirations. They are endearing or silly or naughty or serious or nonsensical. In my own small collection I have many inscrip-tions: Lovely Thomas; My Darling; Forget-me-Not; Dear George; Sweet William; I will for Ever Love the Giver; Be ye

Therefore Ready; Kiss me Quick; Dear Mother; Love me Truely; Love don't be Falce. Spelling is often crazy. There are scores of others: Kiss me Quick my Mome is coming; I love the Boys; Merry me Quick; I wonce loved them that ner loved me; My Hart Hakes for you; My Dear I love you as Birds love Cherries; Sarah Dazeley, Hung 1843. Sarah, who was beautiful and only twenty-two, was a sort of female Bluebeard, knowing that arsenic was the shortest way with husbands.

Just as, in fact, indifference is the shortest way with art. No art ever died of anything but indifference. Art thrives on opposition, even more than oppression, and it has even thrived on stupidity. But it has no response to indifference except death. And it is simply indifference which is killing the art of making lace on pillows, an art which had its heyday in an age which, for all artistic purposes, not to speak of others, we now despise.

All this is, of course, exactly typical of mankind. It is not so much true that familiarity breeds contempt as that it breeds indifference, and after almost four centuries of familiarity with lace-making it is now in the natural order of things that there should be a breeding of indifference. But wait. Give the whole business another ten or twenty years, until the old ladies are mouldering in the churchyards of Ouse and Nene and their precious bobbins and bobbin-winders and parchments are kicking about in the forgotten corners of antique shops, and indifference will suddenly give way to a fashionable yearning to have it all back again. This is one of mankind's oldest tricks: indifference to a thing while it possesses it, then a great howling and crying out for it when the thing has gone. So with lace. In fifty years, unless something remarkable happens, lace-making on pillows will be a memory. Then, unless the girls of that day go naked, which is, of course, very possible, a great sighing and moaning will go up for the lovely work of past days, of, in fact, our own generation.

And Ouse and Nene will, incidentally, have lost the thing which binds them together. It is odd to think of these two rivers, so like threads of water themselves, being bound together for almost four hundred years by threads which were almost as miraculous and delicate as water itself. It is absorbing to think of this metaphorical binding together of two really separate peoples devoted to an art dropped on their doorstep by another country. And, not least, of their adaptation of it: their aspiration toward new designs, the modelling of patterns on the things they loved, tulips and roses and honeycomb and chains and the strange shapes of spiders' webs and even the frost on Victorian window-panes, and the inspired growth of the bobbins, reflecting the crude genius of the people, recording their births and deaths, tears and laughter, jealousy and silliness, in a way that no other art has ever quite accomplished.

Otters and Men

Throughout the writing of this book I have been hoping for an excuse to say something about the otter; and the only excuse I have wanted is the otter itself. The truth is I have never seen an otter; which is perhaps not so odd as it sounds, as I shall show in a moment. I console myself with the fact that otters are mainly nocturnal hunters, that they are very elusive anyway, and with the newly acquired news that otters are living, and breeding, less than a mile from my front door. So I travel hopefully and I have no doubt that I shall, in due course, and when I least expect it and most likely when this book has passed beyond my control, get the sight of my first otter. I hope, most of all, that it will be an unexpected sight. Surprise is more than half the delight of natural sights: the sudden blue cometing of a kingfisher, the red shadow of a fox moving across the land, the plum-coloured glowing of a bullfinch, the uprising of the moths, or a sudden sight of hundreds and hundreds of kingcups burning up from the dark earth of marshes. I once saw a fox moving among a flock of sheep. It was so unexpected and unbelievable that I stood quite still, almost with shock, and while I stood there the fox moved among the sheep exactly like a setter, the flock taking much less notice of him than it would have done of a dog. There was no panic or scuttling or silly flocking together; only a casual uplifting of heads and a momentary staring of wooden faces as the fox came downhill, saucy and quiet as a backyard cat. As he came among the sheep, he looked very brilliant against their dun sluddered wool, and all the time nothing happened at all. Then it was I myself who upset both him and sheep together. I shifted my ground a fraction and he saw me straight away. And the sheep, seeing him look up, looked up themselves, and there we stood, for almost a minute, sheep and fox staring at me as intruder, sheep with silly reared heads ready to bolt, fox sublimely casual and arrogant, until at last he slowly loped off again, dog-like, taking his own time, threading his way among the flock with all the sauce in the world, disappearing finally into a copse of chestnut, the sheep taking no more notice than if he had done it a thousand times before.

All this had the sharp joy of unexpectedness in it. But a week later, at the same spot, I saw it all again: same fox, same sheep, all the same arrogance and sauce as ever, and I have never been able to make up my mind which was the most surprising of these two surprising performances. What I do know is that they gave me, I guarantee, a higher, acuter and finer pleasure than is ever experienced by any hard-riding pink-coat who covers his lust for killing by the excuse that riding to hounds is his only way of freshening his whiskey-ridden liver and, as an afterthought, of giving the fox a little fun.

This kind of fun is, incidentally, one of the reasons why it is so difficult for me, and for that matter anybody else, to get a sight of an otter. Otters are hunted and killed, in England, at something like the rate of four hundred and fifty a year. This is, of course, a small number when you think that Lord X, with party, may dispose of three thousand grouse in a single day, or that Colonel Y, with his famous double two hundred pound-weight punt-gun, may bring down a hundred birds at one discharge. But it means this: that in my short life of thirty years, reckoning at four hundred a year, something like twelve thousand otters have been killed in England for the purpose of fun. How exquisite and long-drawn-out this fun has sometimes been I will show presently. For the moment, since a writer must sometimes give reasons for words he uses, I will explain why I use the word fun and not, let us say, the words public safety, natural history, protection of farmers, or sporting exercise. The otter is a harmless animal. He lives a life in which the amount of his offence towards man can be put in a match-box. It is true that he lives on fish, but so also do herons and wild duck and pike and kingfishers and swans and cats and men and women. But since very few of us ever eat fresh-water fish, the only people who have a genuine grievance against the otter are fishermen. But fishermen are, generally, unvindictive men who go through life nursing, not a grievance against otters, but a fixed and boyish desire to catch fish of fabulous size. If anyone could honestly claim to hunt otters on grounds of revenge, it would be fishermen. But otters are not hunted by fishermen. They are hunted by those people whose notions of fun were satirised by that devastating remark of a famous Frenchman concerning the English: "It's a lovely day. Let's go out and kill something."

Thus, one of the supreme arguments of fox-hunters, that the fox is a pest, carries no weight at all when it comes to otters. Otters are shy, elusive, unsavage creatures, the last remaining water animals of any considerable size in this country. Since they are so unhostile and so inoffensive why, then, are they hunted? And the answer is, of course, for fun.

The question now arises, fun for whom? In fox-hunting the fun is popularly supposed to be equally divided between hunter and hunted. Hunters assure us that the fox enjoys it all. Having also great powers of mobility and cunning, he has chances of escape. The otter's chances of escape are clearly much less; since he is a water mammal, the mobility of his movements is severely restricted. He is safe only in the deepest water.

But these restrictions do not matter. If he cannot be hunted over a wide area, he can at least be hunted for a long time. If to be hunted is fun, then that fun is surely greater if long-drawn-out. It is clear also that hunters themselves are restricted, since the fun is naturally hampered by much messing about in cold water, by the necessity for smoking out the otter with rags of burning paraffin and so on.

Thus, in order to equalise this business of fun, to make it pleasant for otters as well as man, otters are hunted not only for a long time, for seven or eight or ten or even eleven hours at a stretch, but in spring. This is clearly a splendid time. Rivers are then lovely with kingcup and ladysmock, meadows are starred and belled with daisy and cowslip, and above all the female otter is in cub. She may even have given birth to her cubs. But what matter? She is about to be afforded the pleasure, the privilege, of being harried and hunted and having her living guts ripped out by forty human beings, twenty or thirty hounds and some terriers. Spring, the period of gestation and delivery, is perhaps a little awkward for her. But it cannot be helped. She is very lucky, since this same hunt, thinly disguised, is still much occupied with foxes, to be hunted at all. Nor would it be of much use to her to protest, even if she could protest with anything more articulate than the voice of agony and pain, that she had her living cubs in her belly. The fox, too, has cubs in spring, and is it not great fun for the fox also?

Fun is a curious word. It has many meanings and perhaps I misconstrue it? And since I have never seen an otter, except behind the glass of a painted case, who am I to say that the otter does not enjoy the fun of having its belly bloodily ripped? Indeed, I am sure that it does enjoy it, just as a horse, leaping over a fence, enjoys the laceration of its own guts by barbed wire, just as a dog enjoys being half smashed under the wheels of a car, and just as a child would enjoy, let us say, having a limb amputated without an anæsthetic. If you have it one way you must have it another. All flesh is a vehicle of pain.

Pain, too, like fun, is a word of many meanings and it is not surprising, perhaps, that for many people the two things are synonymous. For such people the laceration of an otter's living flesh is an amusing thing. I do not find this in the least hard to believe. Such people would, I think, take pleasure in publicly hanging negroes and burning them after death. What difference, for these people, between the thick-skinned otter and the thick-skinned negro?

But what does astonish me is that the law of this country still allows this rotten and most bloody exhibition of human behaviour. If I were to get up from this chair, arm myself with a stick and beat the nearest dog to the point of death, I should earn the contempt of all decent men and the penalty of the law on top of it in the shape of fines or imprisonment. And no one would question

the justice of it and no one would listen to my pleas that it was sport. Similarly, if a cockney bird-catcher took bullfinches and goldfinches by methods involving pain, and was caught in the act, he would share my fate. But the law of his country, still too often framed on the assumption that property is higher than life, especially if it is the property of the rich and the life of the poor, has no objection, no condemnation and no penalty for those sections of the public who have nothing better to do than to incite one set of animals to rip out the living guts of another. Such repugnant bloodiness in a so-called civilised age and country make me wish, sometimes, that the laws of England could be framed, for a change, behind the walls of a madhouse.

This whole question of pain and wild creatures touches us all. And the best of all laws concerning man and the wild was framed by W. H. Hudson. "Pet nothing," said Hudson, "and persecute nothing." And touching this question, it occurs to me that pity is in every way as contemptible as hatred; by which I mean pity for one creature against its natural enemy and hatred for the creature in pursuit of its natural victim. All this is sentimentalism, which in turn is weakness, which in turn is a breeder of a form of silly cruelty.

I can instance this best by referring to some remarks by a correspondent in a reactionary country newspaper. This gentleman, incensed that I should attack the destruction of many interesting and lovely native creatures for the sake of preserving the alien pheasant, reminded me that the law of nature is "kill or be killed," and had I ever heard of the nasty business of a stoat attacking a rabbit? He was proud to inform me that he had seen this occurrence once. I could not inform him then, but I do inform him

133

now, that I have seen that occurrence many times. But what of it? If the law of nature is "kill or be killed," then both stoat and rabbit are rigidly obeying it. The law of natural instinct is as strong as iron. But all this is not enough for our friend the reactionist. He cannot bear it. The law of "kill or be killed" is all very well on paper, but he cannot bear it in life. It is cruel. In true reactionary fashion, therefore, he runs for his gun, shoots the stoat and with one discharge sets his pained senses at rest.

Now this man is first a fool, and second, and worse, a senti-mentalist. In one breath he exhorts us to remember that the law of nature is "kill or be killed"; in the next he relates how, unable to endure its apparent harshness, he did his best to destroy it by the application of human justice in the form of powder and shot. If this man shoots stoats because they kill rabbits, then, if he is logical —and you see how logical he is—he must also shoot owls because they kill mice, swans because they kill fish, fish because they kill other fish, hawks because they kill sparrows, and, indeed, any creature that kills another for its natural food. He will be excused killing himself only because his own killing will be done in obedience to a man-made and not a natural law. This man's policy of pity and persecution, carried to its logical extreme, would in fact mean his spending his whole life in shooting the strong because they preyed on the weak. He would reply, justly, that such a business were foolish and cruel. Yet this man is very angry with me because I deplore the wholesale massacre of wild creatures by men in order that other men may have the pleasure of shooting half-tame birds.

In support of this anger he produces a stock argument which it is time, I think, was smashed once and for all. Where the fox-hunter argues that if fox-hunting died out the fox would die out also, the shooter argues that if it were not for gamekeepers killing off the beasts and birds of prey we should lose our singing birds. And this is our reactionist's argument.

But he forgets two things. First, that in woods and copses the amount of small-bird life is very very small, whereas, if his argument were true, it ought to be very very large. The simple reason for this is that small birds, among which we number all our singers, build and flourish in other places. They love air and sunlight and the open hedgerow. Any observer can prove this for himself by taking a mile of hedgerow and checking the number of its singing-birds' nests against the number of similar nests in a square mile of woodland. The second thing our reactionist forgets is that all predatory creatures, stoats, weasels, jays, owls, rats, squirrels and so on, are about as thickly distributed over the open country of field and hedgerow as they are through the woodland. Stoats and weasels and rats all prefer nothing so much as a hedgerow for a hunting-ground, where the earth is dry and the weasel can worm along under the dead leaves like a snake. So the

truth is that the keeper, for all the intensity of his activities, only kills a fraction of the great army of predatory creatures. His work is confined, mainly, to woods in general and to those woods in particular where his young pheasants are reared. He does not touch the greater area of open land.

Very astonishing, then, to find that, in the area where the keeper's activities are smallest, the life of singing birds is greatest, and similarly astonishing to find that, in the area where his vigilance is greatest, the life of singing birds is smallest. In short, the belief that a killing of creatures of prey in woodlands automatically preserves the bird-life of the rest of the countryside is, I think, a nonsensical myth. The balance of nature is well able to correct itself, and I believe, with Hudson, that the life of the wild needs neither pity nor persecution for its preservation. No one species needs protection against another. It needs protection only against man.

In my own garden, which is not large, we house an increasing number of nests, tits, linnets, chaffinches, thrushes, hedge-sparrows, blackbirds, starlings, wrens, fly-catchers. We have, at the same time, patrolling the very hedge in which most of these nests are built, a pair of weasels, at least one stoat and probably a pair, some rats and, as visitors, some jays. Such a proximity of opposing forces ought, according to the reactionist, to mean an end of eggs if not also of birds. The plain fact is that we have lost, in three years, one nest of new-hatched blackbirds. And still finches and stoats and linnets and weasels and thrushes and rats live gaily together.

And with Hudson I hold, too, that the best of wild life is seen by those who observe it as they would a drama, with patience and tolerance and without the stupidity of petting or shedding blood. In that drama the tigerish bloodiness of the stoat has just as much place, and is as interesting, as the song of a blackbird; the hovering and swooping and savage descent of a sparrow-hawk is just as much a miracle as the weaving of the nest of the chaffinch. The laws are made and played out inexorably, and with an ultimate perfection of balance. Man, who shoots stoats because they feed on rabbits and who finds pleasure in the raw ripped-open bellies of otters, is the discordant force.

Of shooters, in fact, I saw only one, in my life, who ever touched me to pity. He used to come along the high road above the Nene on fine winter afternoons. He came in the attitude of a man stalking prey. Suddenly he would stop and start and raise his eyes skyward and very slowly lift a gun that was not there. Then, after taking aim at a bird which was not there either, he shot. Bang! he would shout. Then he would leap about, jubilant, waving his hat with one hand and his imaginary gun with the other. And then, laughing softly, he would creep forward in the grass, with a kind of seraphic stealth, and pick up his bird. Then he would tuck it under his arm and look about him to see if he were being watched. And finally, carrying invisible gun and bird, he would creep off along the road with the strangely happy stealth of lunacy.

That idiot had the best of two worlds. He shot, but he never hit. He killed but never pained. He shot, also, birds which no one else ever shot or ever even saw. With that crazy gun he might, for all I know, have brought down pelicans and peacocks and birds of paradise.

The Rivers of England

In such a small country as England, where almost every village is within shouting distance of the next and where towns sit on each other's doorsteps, we are all bound up with streams of some kind. Rivers and their tributaries snake across the country as thick as veins on a leaf. The island shape of the land, and its narrowness, has made it possible for rivers to rise within a mile or two of each other and yet flow in exactly opposite directions. Rivers all over the land almost join each other. They twist to avoid each other, run parallel with each other, blunder against each other. The land is even split up by rivers, here and there, into small inland islands, as the Isle of Oxney in Kent. The number of twiddling little streams in England is fantastic. They look, on the map, less like the veins on a leaf than a jumble of black snakes with their heads drinking at the sea. And not more than a tenth of them, I suppose, are navigable except by the adventurous, by pain of punt-poles. In such a country as America not more than half a dozen English rivers would, I suppose, be called rivers at all. That vast country would scorn the infantile paps from which most of the meadows of England draw suck. The fierceness of American summers would frizzle up their dribbles of milk, like batter on a red-hot grid. Thames, from which at least ten million of us draw life, would find a place of respect, and with it Tyne and Trent and Tees and Severn. The rest would be less than playgrounds for the sailing of paper boats.

Yet these many small rivers are, in England, extremely precious. It is they who are responsible, primarily, for the moulding of the face of the land. With hills, they are the land's original features. We are inclined to forget this, to see the land as having been, always, a piece of ready-made architecture, complete in itself, completely finished, neatly decked with the red and grey of towns, the nest-coloured villages, the rule-divided fields, the dark sectors of woodland. Whereas the original shape of the land, as far as you can get down to it and if you can get down to it at all, must have had no outstanding features but the hills and these small despised rivers and the spread of forest and marsh. And since civilisation has tended to widen rivers rather than diminish them, there must have been a day when Thames and Severn had less nobility of breadth even than now, and when Nene and Bure and Test and Stour and so on were like a jumble of gentle worms.

Yet all the beauty of these streams lies in their pastoral smallness and gentleness. They have the same unpretentious loveliness as their unfanciful monosyllabic names. And what curious mechanism of circumstances, anyway, coined these names? From Tyne to Thames and Thames to Taw and Taw up to Tweed, the rivers of England share a collection of sturdy, quaint, almost comic names equalled only by one other section of names in the language, and that, oddly enough, of the fish which swim in them. These stumpy little names are not confined to one county or coast. They are common to the whole seaboard. They are even repeated. So that there are a whole handful of Stours and Ouses and Avons. And it would be hard to find, I think, another collection of such laconic, almost crusty monosyllables. The names of English villages form a line of buttery syllables that have in them, often, the very taste of the much-watered, very green English countryside. It is as though their names had been churned out of the cream of the landscape. That butteriness is tasted in names like Collyweston, Fotheringhay, Stoke Bruerne, Moreton Pinkney, Weedon Lois, Silverstone, Sibbertoft and Yelvertoft, which are all, it so happens, names from one tiny section of the land, the country about the Nene. In other parts they grow richer perhaps, or softer, or creamier, or even sourer, so that there are names like bits of strong crumbly cheese, harsh on the tongue, with a sour strength in them. Such names as Hanging Houghton, Yardley Gobion, Furtho, Cold Higham, Tansor, Glapthorn, Blatherwycke, Shutlanger, Old, which are again, as it happens, names from the country of the Nene. The names of hills and woods and fields have evolved out of the same rich ingredients of fancy and earth, as their names tell. Of hills: Strawberry Down, Pincushion Hill, Shap, Love's Hill, Bredon Hill, Snowdon, from small to great. Of woods: Pesthouse Wood, Buttockspice Wood, Silley Coppice, St. Mary's Wood, Porter's Coppice, Nobottle Wood, Skulking Dudley Coppice, Lady Copse. Of fields: Dark Closes, Vine Hills, Cat's Brain, Whorestone Furlong, Dead Shells, Lammas Mead, Deedman's Grave, Windesarse, Red and White Starch. And since farms are bound up with hills and woods and fields, the names of farms also break out into the same homely and delicious poetry: Prince Rupert's Farm, Powder Blue Farm, Magpie Farm, Buttermilk Hall. Even the names of ponds and springs follow the same delightful pattern: Saffron Moat, Pottosy Pond, Cat's Water, Red Link. And even the names of roads: Salt Way, Watling Street, Ickneild Way, Car Dike, King's Meadow Lane. A man without any knowledge of the origins of his native tongue can feel in these names a creamy delicacy, a sturdy strength, a rough wantonness, as the case may be. They are rich with the colour and taste of the land.

But what has happened to the names of rivers? Where fields and farms and hills and ponds and even roads are named so richly, it would seem the most natural thing for the names of rivers to follow the same tradition. They might at any rate have revealed some benevolence of colour or similarity of sound or some air of pastoral tranquillity in keeping with the streams themselves. Thus, juggling with the names, we might have had Powder Blue River, Saffron River, Dead Shells River, the River St. Mary. Breaking away from that tradition, keeping closer to the life of rivers themselves, we might have had Swan River, Lily River, or, preserving that tradition of proper vulgarity which has always been so strong a feature of English rural fancy, River Windesarse. Such names belong as rightly and surely to English countryside as campion and dandelion, as rook and blackbird, fox and otter, or better still to that tradition of old flower-names which our more proper, gentlemanly, otter-ripping age has strangled out of usage.

But the names of rivers pursue a course of independence which is baffling. Where we might expect River Swan or River Nine

Springs, we have Ouse and Nene, names which not only look mysterious but which are mysterious. Of Nene we have, it seems, no satisfactory etymological explanation. My assumption of Nine, for Nine Springs, is based only on local hearsay. The name has gone, in ten centuries, through some changes: Nyn, Nien, Neene, Ene, Nine, but has never really changed its crusty monosyllabic mould. And still, in this age of light, we are as much in the dark as to its meanings as ever. Ouse would seem to have been Use, Usan, Wusan, thus breaking its monosyllabic rule a little, but still keeping close to that tradition of rough and seemingly uninspired brevity which governs the naming of almost all the rivers of this island.

Those names seem often, in fact, less like names of rivers than of prehistoric beasts, as in Usk and Swale and Bure and Stort and Jaw, or the syllables of some nonsense rhyme, as in Wensum and Yare and Swale and Idle, Tweed and Tees and Tyne and Test; or the names of crabbed women, as in Till and Tamar, or even of birds and birds now lost as in Dove and Parret and Kennet, Nidd and Aire. These are names, with one or two exceptions, which would seem to have no other place in the language, to belong exclusively and peculiarly to these rivers. Etymologists, no doubt, will explain them, which does not explain away at all their abrupt crudity, their bluff oddity of look and sound.

Only very occasionally does this long pattern break into easier colour and softer sound. Then we get Severn and Avon, only to find that Avon means nothing more than river, and Windrush and Cherwell, only to find that Cher is wrapped in mystery and that Well (O.E. Wielle) means nothing more than stream. And we get, more rarely still, some name that clings to the pattern-

edge like a piece of French embroidery, too delicate, some name like Coquet or Eden or Isis, altogether out of place in that rough stitchery.

But perhaps, after all, such an odd and unembroidered pattern of names is right. Rivers, unlike fields and farms and wood and hills, are not local. Thompson's Farm will do very well for those within a fox-bark of its door, but beyond the parish boundaries it will be a mere piece of empty picturesqueness. Whorestone Furlong will have meaning perhaps, for those who are near enough and old enough to know something of the history of the girl who stamped on it the mark of her profession, but it will not do at all in some other place where, perhaps, ladies are and always have been more virtuous. And if such a name, coined by a sturdier and less veneered people, had become the name of the mother river, in place of Thames, it would, no doubt, have given offence to more respectable ages and might conceivably have had to be changed by Act of Parliament, though there will be some who would support it as being appropriate to a city whose population of prostitutes is unrivalled in the world.

So it is right, perhaps, that rivers should not bear, like other country places, the imprint of some local fancy or, more especially, of some local fancy lady. They require, since they are such far-reaching, general features of the landscape, some more universal name, a name that will be common to both source and mouth, that will serve equally well the cowmen of its middle meadows, the dockers of its ports, the clerks walking over its bridges, the fishermen angling on its banks, the lovers watching its water-lilies in the July sun. Such a name as Nene, seeming to mean nothing, is aloof, uncontroversial. It is above local pettiness. It binds a whole section of the land together. If rivers had been named according to local imagination, streams would have been split up into the pettiness of parishes. As it is, they remain single forces, common inheritances under common names. They are at once independent and universal.

All of which still does not explain that string of odd river names, with its Usk and Ouse and Till and Tamar, Nidd and Nene and Ware and Wensum, running round the coast of England like some necklace of primitive and crusty stone and bead.

Down to the Sea

The fusing of river and sea is sometimes a dull affair. Where there ought to be some grand effect, some turbulent seething together of the two waters in final consummation, too often a river creeps into the sea, muddily and shabbily, tin cans floating, the rim of tide-wash scummed jaggedly over iron-coloured sand; or is even imprisoned, sometimes, in the back-alley culverts of seaside towns, fish-stinking, nothing but a dull spew of unwanted water. It is only the great rivers and those small fiery streams that hurl themselves whitely down cliffs that make anything like a noble effect. It is the expectation of the thing that is entrancing: the widening of the stream, the increase of boats and cargoes, the flattening of the land, the increasing width of the sky and that strange effect of the sky's loftiness, marvellously aloof and far-off and pure as though sea-washed, as it hangs in the flat distance above the sea.

There is some phase here, just before the last, when rivers have some removed and indefinable beauty, a quality of detached solitude. Flowing broadly on wide marshes cut up into crazy dyke sections of sea-stunted grass, with their dumb population of sheep, they seem to belong neither to sea nor earth. Widening themselves, they reflect also the new width of the sky, with the result, often, that they create an effect of emptiness, at once forlorn and fascinating. If they are tidal and not only tidal but small, like the Rother, they have the air, at low tide, of having given up the ghost of life altogether. Their waters shrink to a petty sand-coloured trickle, leaving the bare banks swelling up on either side like sulky breasts of sand, the shipping high and heeled-over on the narrow bits of shore. The sea sucks out the river's strength, leaving only that weak and ridiculous width of water, no more than a brook. And then, at high tide, when it gives it back, the result is almost a kind of cheating, a trick-miracle. The bare breasts of sand are swallowed up, the brim of water rises, and the new width spreads out, finally, between the broken crusts of the spear-grassed banks with unbelievable strength and depth and dignity, and the ships that looked as though wrecked begin to float again with an air of permanent serenity, of having been there for ever.

Red-sailed, bearing chiefly cargoes of coal and corn-yellow timber, these small ships are the proper links that bind together river and sea. Built for each, they owe something and in turn give something to each. Ships are, in one sense, and perhaps a very natural sense, like trees; they uplift a scene, give it dignity and a new enchantment of perspective. A fleet of small ships, with sails furled and masts and spars bare against the sky, is like the sea-ghost of a spinney. So, on the last reaches of a river there is nothing so enchanting, except the flowers which I shall come to in a moment, as the small red-sailed spinneys of ships lying by the woodyards, unloading, or beached on the steep sand-breasts, as though storm-broken, waiting for the tide. They give the river an utterly fresh smack of life, salty, in some way foreign and yet natural, and in the best sense of the word romantic.

And like them, the last flowers of the river belong, properly, to both sea and land or rather to the continuation of them, the marsh. In the desolate acres of the Romney shingle foxgloves make great pink companies all summer, seeding and blossoming where there seems to be no substance or earth at all; blue dwarf anchusa comes later, and with it, near the coast, that glorious golden sea-poppy, with its almost sea-coloured leaves, the flower less like a poppy than some yellow flower-shell; and with them, all summer, every-where, along the marsh roadsides, in the shingle, to wherever the salt in the air reaches, the countless tussocks of sea-pink, like small pink bobbles in flower, like small coronets of gauze in seed. And less general, but more lovely, spreading only a short way inland, the little blue shrubs of sea-thistle, like powder-blue holly, almost silvery, shining like fierce frozen bits of blue-silver sea. And always, clinging close to the river itself and the dykes, the great strips and clumps of flowering reed, like stout corn, feather-eared, which colour to straw and fawn in autumn and remain all winter, feathers growing more and more like the old matted wool of sheep, reeds more and more like some too abundant storm-smashed crop of unmown and unwanted corn.

But as the river widens finally, flowers are subsidiary, more immaterial embroideries. They are no longer part of it, as in the middle reaches, where the course was lily-locked and the only sails were pennants of wild iris flapping in the little serene summer winds. The river itself has grown detached, as if the inevitability of it all had become a little tiresome. Its true character, its independence of beauty, is dropping away. The sea draws it on and down and finally under, in absolute subjugation, draining the strength of its waters like some too-greedy never satisfied lover. The river is, at last, to be a victim itself of the inexorable magnetism of water. From the source downwards all its turns and prettiness and growth and character have in reality been subservient to this exercise of the sea's magnetism. Its end was resolved before it began. A road may go to any one of a thousand places: to the tops of hills, to towns, to solitary farm-houses, to the summits of mountains, anywhere. But a river, snaking to all points of the compass, has only one destination and one end.

And in the perpetual obedience to this never-shifting purpose lies, I think, some of the secret of the fascination of rivers: the fascination of the inevitable. We are attracted very greatly by the unknown, by the mystery of things in general and not least of ourselves in particular. But the fascination of the inevitable, the foreseen growth or destruction or changing or dying of some object or living thing, is immense. The inevitability of death attracts us all into a state of wonder and terror. And in some such way we stand fascinated by the river's end, foreseen, inevitable as night and day. Standing on the small bridges of brooks, setting sail the paper boats, watching the dash of mill-races, the storm of currents, we look forward continually to one point: the final moment of subjugation, the end, the supreme point of fusion that is, in a way, a kind of death. We look forward and think forward, in fascination, always to the sea.

And having arrived, having reached the ultimate moment, what happens? We at once begin to look forward no more, but back.

Having reached the point of fusion, we no longer want it. We look back instead to the middle reaches, the small beginnings. We see the broad placid reaches of meadow and water, the skin of quicksilver shining up almost painfully in the straight-sunned afternoons, the quiet play of fish and dragonfly, the visionary almost nun-whiteness of the water-lilies, the showering down of poplar catkins like some woolly hatching out of many maroon caterpillars on the spring water, the landmarks of bridge and pub and ferry and mill, the white comedies of ducks, the washing of sheep in shallow places on summer mornings, the pencilled images of fishermen, the narrowing down and not the widening out of water, the clarifying, the gradual going back to smallness and delicacy, to the small ripple of water like a bubbling of white wine on the white stones and white strips of sand in brooks, to the small fish motionless in shadow-crowds in the small brook pools, the small pink patter of crab petals on bank and stream, the small but startling plop of voles in the small but deep silences, the last narrowing back to the first fierce uprising of water, crystalline, insignificant, like some bubbling up of melting ice, the spring and beginning of things.